TOKYO
street food

Tom Vandenberghe, Luk Thys, Miho Shibuya & Tomoko Kaji

CONTENTS

- **6**   Introduction
- **10**   About
- **12**   About this book
- **15**   Locations (+ overview recipes)
- **15**   Tokyo
- **16**   Osaka
- **18**   Fukuoka
- **19**   ...and beyond!

TOM'S STORY

- **21**   Mission ramen
- **44**   Izakaya in Kyoto
- **62**   Team-building Japan
- **75**   Fukuoka – The home of tonkotsu
- **84**   Ramen noodle bar
- **114**   On the road
- **137**   Eat 'till you drop
- **180**   Tokyo food crawl
- **192**   A chef's table

TOMOKO AND MIHO

- **24**   Good food and lots of laughter
- **33**   Miso
- **100**   Bento
- **107**   Sake and shochu
- **133**   Okonomiyaki: Hiroshima-Yaki and Osaka-Yaki
- **142**   The shopping street Tenjinbashisuji Shotengai
- **164**   Izakaya and tachinomiya

THE BASICS

- **196**   Dashi
- **198**   Cooked rice
- **199**   Sushi rice and katsuobushi salt
- **200**   Chicken stock and vegetarian ramen stock
- **202**   Eggs in soy sauce, marinated bamboo shoots and gyoza dipping sauce
- **203**   Marinated braised pork, shiitake-seaweed butter and tonkatsu sauce
- **204**   Shiodare, Misodare, Basildare and Tantandare
- **206**   Sweetened adzuki beans

- **208**   The Japanese language
- **210**   Addresses
- **214**   Index

INTRODUCTION

Street food in Japan: you don't immediately think of streets and squares full of food carts or pavements decked with tables and chairs... The country with the most Michelin stars in the world is associated mainly with sushi and sashimi and seldom, if ever, with street food. But this is wrong because sushi used to be street food; it was sold in *yatai* or mobile food stalls.

Nowadays, you can still find those yatai at religious festivals – the main religions are Buddhism and Shinto – and other events where lots of people gather. They are still a popular attraction. But there's much more to it than that, except that street food is not always as visible in Japanese public life. It's almost as if it's not done to be seen eating on the street, so people do their utmost to hide it away. Often, you have to look in alleys or under railway bridges, very often close to stations. But once you know where to look, you'll discover a laid-back and cheaper way of eating that really brings you into contact with Japanese people, which also means a little bit closer to Japanese culture.

I only have to think about Japan and automatically I smell the typical odour of *dashi*, a stock made from roasted, finely-ground slivers of bonito – a type of tuna (*katsuobushi*). If I had to name one type of food preparation that characterises Japanese cooking, it would be dashi, much more so than sushi or sashimi. You can find these bonito flakes at any supermarket and dashi forms the base for many soups and dipping sauces. That characteristic smell can't be found anywhere else in the world. Dashi is the absolute key to Japanese cooking.

Ask any chef in the world about his favourite country for eating out and nine times out of ten the answer will be "Japan". Japanese cuisine has its own unique identity as well as many external influences. The most significant influence, as is the case in the rest of Asia, comes from Chinese cuisine: ramen noodles are originally Chinese. Rice and soy sauce became part of everyday fare via Korea. English sailors introduced (Madras) curry from India, their former colony. Then the French familiarised the Japanese with *croquettes* (*korokke*) and, in turn, the Portuguese also made their mark: they introduced tempura, as well as bread (*pan*) and many types of sweets. Japan has four large islands: Hokkaido, Honshu, Shikoku and Kyushu. The country has different climate zones, ranging from very cold in the north (Hokkaido) to subtropical in the south (Kyushu). Of course, the climate influences the various regional types of cuisine.

Washoku or traditional Japanese cuisine, is on UNESCO's list of intangible cultural heritage, and with good reason. Restaurants in Japan often specialise in one thing, which therefore becomes their strength. A true master specialises in one trade, in some cases for his whole life. A craftsman, or *shokunin*, is a highly prized person in Japan.

Restaurants are literally stacked one on top of another, often without English signs, and are therefore not always easily accessible or easy to find. A five-storey building can contain ten different restaurants, each only the size of two snooker tables, with room for about a dozen people. Space is scarce in Japan. But this makes it more convenient for the *shokunin*: with only twelve seats rather than twenty-four, he can really indulge his customers' tastes and serve up pure quality.

The Japanese have a special feel for cleanliness and style – it's as if everyone comes out of a box. Their desire for balance and their unparalleled yearning for perfection also explain the abundance of starred restaurants. But what makes Japanese cuisine so special is the deep desire for detail – and cooking is all about the detail. Presentation, experience, that little bit extra: these all make a difference. Often, a link also exists between the presentation of dishes and the changing seasons.

In addition to a gourmet meal in a restaurant – the most chic restaurants often don't even have a sign outside – you can also choose to eat in a more casual or relaxed manner. Traditional *yatai* or food carts may have somewhat lost their significance in high- end, futuristic cities like Tokyo, but they are still just numerous enough to play an important role. Cheap lunch concepts such as *donburi, udon, soba, tori* or *tonkatsu* eateries are well-represented all over Japan. But there is so much more: *tachinomiya* or standing bars make Japan unique; here you you can eat the most incredible things while standing up. *Izakaya* is a fantastic, low-threshold food and drink concept that bears a striking resemblance to tapas bars. As if that were not enough, train stations and transport hubs serve up a feast for any traveller on a culinary voyage of discovery: the colourful *ekiben* boxes at stations look almost psychedelic. If you're feeling a little adventurous, the market street or shopping arcade offers an incredible variety of street food, from delis to croquette bars, tofu shops and funky bakeries. Convenience stores, such as 7-Eleven, Lawson's or FamilyMart, offer even more accessible solutions to bridge the hunger gap at any time of day. No other country in the world has 24-hour shops that provide such high-quality snacks.

Japan amazes and continues to amaze. Forget all the clichés about light and healthy because Japanese street food cuisine breathes rock 'n' roll and a hearty dose of fat. Let yourself go with the mayonnaise topping, a steaming bowl of ramen noodles or a portion of *okonomiyaki*, the true cholesterol explosions! These dishes emerged after the Second World War, at a time of great scarcity, when a crafty America sold grain to Japan to feed its needy population.

What I still miss about Japan, as well as the food, is the courtesy and the politeness of its people. Wherever you go, you are greeted with a cheery *"konnichi wa"* (hello), *"ohayo gozaimasu"* (good morning), *"komban wa"* (good evening), or you are thanked with a friendly *"arigato"*. That is incredibly infectious: I really miss the etiquette each time I come back to the West. There's a good chance that a visit to Japan will make the same impression on you; what is certain is that it will be one of the best culinary experiences of your life. *Itadakimasu!*

ABOUT

TOM

Kookstudio Eetavontuur was Tom Vandenberghe's very first project. In an industrial building in Ghent, which he rented from Luk Thys and Foodphoto, he taught people how to use new ingredients. Ten years ago, working with his then-girlfriend, Eva Verplaetse, and his partner in crime, Luk Thys, he published his first recipe book: *Bangkok Street Food*.
Following culinary detours through Vietnam, Singapore, Malaysia and New York, Tom and a group of amazing co-workers opened their first restaurant, the Ramen noodle bar in home port Ghent.

He got to know Tomoko and Miho when they attended a Japanese workshop at Kookstudio Eetavontuur. Sometime later, they jointly organized an izakaya evening at Ramen noodle bar. When he also took a Japanese language immersion course with Tomoko *(sensei)*, their friendship grew, as well as the idea of creating a cookbook together.

The Japanese like to give presents. Miho gave him a hand-made, lovingly prepared bowl of *natto* (fermented soy beans) as a gift. Miho and Tomoko simply cannot understand why he thinks this is delicious, so they refer to him as the strange Belgian.

LUK

Luk is an experienced and well-known food and travel photographer with an international clientele. Many of his pictures are created in his daylight studios in Ghent, where he collaborates with a team of talented photographers and food stylists.

Tom Vandenberghe is his *soul brother*. Together, they roam the globe in search of the ultimate street food stories and pictures. Japan was a source of inspiration in every respect, which further sharpened their appetites for street food.

TOMOKO

Tomoko was born and raised in Osaka, and she's proud of it. About twenty years ago she came to Belgium to study and even during her student years, friends and acquaintances would regularly ask her to cook "something Japanese" for them. Since providing culinary pleasure is one of her great joys in life, a couple of years ago she decided to set up the catering company GOHAN, together with Miho, with a special emphasis on family-style cooking, the "Japanese everyday fare". In so doing, she wants to show that there is so much more to Japanese cuisine than just sushi.

Tomoko is also involved in organising the Japan Square film festival in Ghent, introducing contemporary Japanese culture through film.

MIHO

Miho grew up in a family that ate together every day. All kinds of small dishes were spread out on the table, with over thirty different ingredients. Miho therefore learned to appreciate a wide range of flavours from a very early age. Her inspiration and her passion for food were further stimulated when she went out to eat in Tokyo, often with colleagues, at a typical izakaya or one of the many other eateries. She followed her future husband to Belgium, where she obtained her chef's diploma at the prestigious Spermalie in Bruges. Recently, Miho and her best friend Tomoko launched the catering company GOHAN in Ghent. There, they work to order using both Japanese and local ingredients and techniques.

ABOUT THIS BOOK

It's your first visit to Japan, so what do you do? Point to the plastic food in the window of a restaurant or at your neighbour's plate and say, "I'll have that"? It can work but it might also cost you 100 euros. It's always a bit of a guessing game.

Everyone knows Japan from sushi. Everyone is also convinced that travelling and eating in Japan is expensive – too expensive. I want to use this book to demonstrate that Japan is much more than stylish and chic and expensive and distant. Sushi used to be a street food, a quick take-away snack. But there is still plenty of street food in Japan. In fact, food there is even cheaper than it is here – unless you specifically want to eat dishes cooked by sushi masters or wagyu beef, of course.

Despite its title, *Tokyo Street Food,* this has become a culinary tour of the whole of Japan. We have not confined ourselves to one city for this book. Of course, Tokyo itself is worth an entire encyclopaedia dedicated to street food, but we will leave that task to top experts. What we have created here is a modest but colourful look at street food in Tokyo and in other food destinations, such as Fukuoku and Osaka. The recipes we have included in this book are our interpretations of those preparations, which is precisely where the fun lies in cooking: in experimenting with ingredients and cooking methods.

In 2016 Belgium and Japan celebrated 150 years of diplomatic relations. This book was also a major collaborative effort between Belgium and Japan. Miho was primarily responsible for the recipes, Tomoko for the background information and, as always, I contribute my experiences to Tom's story.

During the summer of 2016 I got to know two amazing people – Miho and Tomoko. They have Japanese cooking in their genes. Our meeting proved to be a huge blessing, not only in culinary terms. It was as if they were sent from heaven. Without Tomoko's and Miho's knowledge, enthusiasm and sophistication, we could never have produced this book.

Ramen noodle bar had celebrated five years, Eetavontuur ten years and my new restaurant Haven was about to open its doors. Autumn of 2016 seemed the ideal time to fly to Japan with the staff and to introduce the team to ramen noodles as they should be. The quest for more knowledge for the Ramen noodle bar was what really brought me to Japan for the first time. Much more so than the other street food books that we published in this series, this has become the story of our own restaurant, Ramen. This fact together with the crazy food trip with our colleagues and meeting Miho and Tomoko resulted in an unforgettable story and in a fantastic collaboration, the results of which you are now holding in your hands.

LOCATIONS (+ OVERVIEW RECIPES)

In contrast to our previous books, we explored more than one city. That means that we did not confine ourselves to Tokyo alone, but also branched out to Osaka and Fukuoka – and justifiably so. These cities offer genuine added value in terms of street food in Japan. The recipes on these pages are listed by location. You can find them listed alphabetically in the index at the back of the book.

TOKYO

With 37 million inhabitants, Tokyo is the futuristic, super-modern capital of the future. Tokyo is not really one city, but a collection of 23 special districts (central Tokyo), surrounded by conurbations. In 1923, Tokyo was hit by one of the strongest earthquakes in Japan's history. Over 140,000 people lost their lives and many traditional neighbourhoods were flattened. Initially, the city's name was Edo. In 1869, it became the capital of Japan, where the emperor resided. Alongside London and New York, Tokyo is now one of the world's largest financial centres. It offers science fiction street scenes, neon lights, a pop culture mecca, a night life like no other, etc.

The renowned Tsukiji market, located on Tokyo Bay, is a microcosm in itself and one of the city's major attractions. Rumours have been circulating for some time that the market could move to a new location. Tokyo has one of the highest concentrations of restaurants in the world with infinite variety; in Tokyo you can order absolutely any dish you can imagine. Central Tokyo, and Ginza in particular, is the sushi centre of the world. It is one big food-fest. The city with the most Michelin stars in the world serves up the best fish you'll ever taste.

27	Breaded chicken *Chicken Katsu*
28	Ice-cold soba noodles with dipping sauce *Zaru soba*
31	Octopus balls *Takoyaki*
34	Cucumber with spicy miso dip *Morokyu*
37	Japanese curry with vegetables *Yasai curry*
38	Miso soup with clams *Asari no misoshiru*
41	Fishcake with corn *Tomorokoshi no satsuma-age*
42	Sushi balls topped with fish *Nigiri sushi*
183	Green soy bean shake *Edamame shake*
184	Scampi burger *Ebikatsu burger*
187	Rice with sea bream sashimi and hot dashi *Tai chazuke*
189	Hand-rolled rice balls with salmon *Sake no onigiri*
190	Grilled mackerel with sea salt *Saba no shioyaki*
195	Karaage-don (rice bowl) with salsa *Salsa sosu no karaage don*

OSAKA

Osaka is the third largest city in Japan and, like Tokyo, is located on the island of Honshu. Osaka was very briefly the capital of Japan, shortly before neighbouring Nara acquired that title. It was then known as Naniwa, a name that is still regularly used. Osaka was heavily bombed during the Second World War, which led *Lonely Planet* to describe it has having little real charm. However, its charm lies in its people. Osaka receives nowhere near the same number of visitors as Tokyo. Over the centuries, it has always been a centre of trade and definitely of food too. Precisely as a result of its "underdog" reputation, the people of Osaka are perhaps more open or more welcoming than those in Tokyo. In Osaka, people are less punctual than in other cities in Japan, you have the feeling that there are greater possibilities there. Flashy skyscrapers, chic neighbourhoods right next to ghetto-like neighbourhoods, rich and poor side-by-side, it just feels more free and easy.

Local street food dishes such as *okonomyaki*, *takoyaki* and *kushikatsu* have their roots here. The counterbalance to the lively street food culture is found in the *kappa* food concept, up-market dining at a restaurant counter. Osaka has more Michelin stars than Paris, for example. By day, its population doubles as a result of people coming to work in Osaka and it becomes the second largest city in Japan. But Osaka really comes to life at night, when the locals come out to eat, drink and be merry. "*Kuidaore*": eat until you drop, is a frequently-heard saying in the city.

Osaka is also very well-known for its comedians, who often move to Tokyo and its major TV studios once they become successful. Osaka (and, by extension, the entire Kansai region to which the city belongs) has a very special feel for humour and an immediately recognisable intonation. Once they have made a breakthrough and moved to Tokyo, these comedians do not modify their dialect at all, instead they make it even more obvious.

65	Triangular breaded chicken sandwich *Chicken katsu sando*
140	Thinly sliced beef with egg *Gyuniku no tamago-toji*
145	Steak with Japanese savoury sauce *Gyu steeki wafu-sosu*
146	Cold green tea *Tsumetai ryokucha*
149	Shaved ice with green tea syrup *Matcha kakigori*
150	Monaka with mascarpone *Mascarpone no monaka*
151	Japanese green tea latte *Matcha latte*
153	Smoked eggs *Kunsei tamago*
154	Japanese-style croquettes with minced meat *Niku korokke*
157	Soy milk pudding *Tonyu purin*
158	Okra and chicken salad *Okura to toriniku no salada*
161	European/Dutch-style aubergines (eggplant) *Nasu no orandani*
162	Japanese omelette *Dashimaki tamago*
167	Rice with hijiki seaweed *Hijiki gohan*
169	Miso-marinated and baked salmon *Sake no saikyo yaki*
170	Pork and kimchi stir-fry *Buta kimchi*
173	Fried rice and noodles *Sobameshi*
174	Sweet and sour pork *Subuta*
177	Savoury Japanese pancakes with cabbage (Osaka-style) *Okonomiyaki (Osaka-style)*
178	Crab and scallops with ponzu *Kani to hotate no ponzu gake*

FUKUOKA

This bustling and eminently liveable city is sometimes referred to as Tokyo's little brother and is Japan's sixth city. Fukuoka grew out of two cities: Fukuoka and Hakata. The oldest part of the city still bears the original name of Hakata.

Fukuoka is the city where the largest number of *yatai*, or food carts, roll out every day to feed the appetites of hungry visitors. In most Japanese cities, yatai have completely disappeared from street life. Fukuoka is the exception and the last trace of a lively and traditional street food culture. Until ten years ago there were still three hundred yatai; now there are only one hundred and fifty. The number of yatai falls every year. Since they are supposedly a nuisance, they are now resisted. I can only hope that they will survive. You have to be in the districts of Tenjin or Nagahama to really get to know the amazing yatai street food culture.

This bustling city is located on the island of Kyushu and enjoys a mild climate. It is the home base of the famous Softbank Hawks baseball team and apparently the most beautiful Japanese women come from Fukuoka. In culinary terms, it is the source of *tonkotsu* ramen stock, *motsunabe*, a local speciality made from pork or beef tripe and *mentaiko* (marinated pollock roe), a commonly-used ingredient.

- 79 Deep-fried skewered meat and vegetables *Kushikatsu*
- 80 Fried skewered chicken *Yakitori (negima)*
- 83 Daikon, egg and fishcake in stock *Oden*
- 88 Ramen with pork stock *Tonkotsu ramen*
- 91 Omelette on fried rice *Omuraisu*
- 92 Sashimi on rice bowl *Kaisen-don*
- 95 Sardines with ginger *Iwashi no nitsuke*
- 96 Spinach with sesame sauce *Horenso no gomaae*
- 99 Meatballs in sweet sauce *Nikudango no ankake*
- 103 Potato salad *Poteto salada*
- 104 Cod roe tempura with perilla leaves *Mentaiko to shiso no tempura*
- 111 Pesto ramen *Basil ramen*
- 113 Dipping noodles *Tsukemen*
- 120 Fried and steamed dumplings *Gyoza*
- 123 Japanese sponge cake *Kasutera*
- 124 Curry bread with beef *Curry pan*

...AND BEYOND!

OKAYAMA
- **66** Vegetables with "broken" tofu *Yasai no shiraae*
- **69** Don (rice bowl) with yuba and thick dashi sauce *Yuba no donburi*
- **70** Cold tofu with various types of garnish *Hiyayakko*
- **73** Udon noodles with oysters *Kaki udon*

KYOTO
- **48** Ramen with spicy minced meat *Tantanmen*
- **51** Pickled Chinese cabbage *Hakusai no tsukemono*
- **52** Thick pancakes with sweetened adzuki beans *Dorayaki*
- **55** Marinated and fried chicken *Tori no karaage*
- **56** Grilled scallops with soy sauce and butter *Hotate no grill*
- **59** Tofu balls with thick dashi sauce *Tofu-dango no ankake*
- **60** Grilled aubergine with bonito flakes *Yaki nasu*

HIROSHIMA
- **126** Steamed bun *Nikuman*
- **129** Cake with sweetened adzuki beans *Taiyaki*
- **130** Japanese-style grilled eel / conger eel *Unagi / anago no kabayaki*
- **134** Savoury Japanese pancakes with cabbage (Hiroshima-style) *Okonomiyaki (Hiroshima-yaki)*

GHENT
- **87** Vegetarian ramen *Vege ramen*

MISSION RAMEN

My very first trip to Japan? That was at the beginning of the new millennium. It was the middle of winter and I can still remember very clearly how cold it was in Tokyo. I was immediately struck by how clean everything was, and how quiet, you could barely hear car engines running. I set out, completely overwhelmed by this new environment, in search of rotating heated toilet seats, Sumo wrestlers and the best sushi in the world. At that time, Japanese streets had far fewer signs written in English than they do now, so that first time I really was "lost in translation". Restaurateurs in Japan are used to displaying plastic food in their windows. It doesn't always look appetising but it was often the only way of knowing, "Hey, this is a restaurant!" Sometimes you had to order ramen noodles from a vending machine at the entrance, feeding in coins and making a selection, which is a hopeless task when you don't know any Japanese.

My then girlfriend, Eva, and I travelled as backpackers and we were not on a generous budget. Still, we quickly found great cheap lunch ideas and we did well on **breaded chicken** (chicken katsu) or **chilled buckwheat noodles with dipping sauce** (zaru soba). The presumption that Japan would be expensive and that you can only find high-end food went straight out the window. We had to search a little but we quickly found our feet and zoomed around the country on the efficient metro and train network. When we were looking for somewhere to sleep in Takayama (we were going to sample the local beef) and had not booked in advance, the hotel was up in arms. The Japanese do not like the unexpected.

Something else that will stay with me forever is my first experience with onsen, Japanese bath houses. It was so cold in our ryokan (traditional Japanese hotel) that Eva and I went to these onsen as often as possible. Men and women are segregated but at least we weren't cold in those hot baths!

Inspired by the film, *Jiro Dreams of Sushi*, I went to Tokyo a second time about three years ago, on my own. Ramen, my noodle bar, had already been open a couple of years but I felt I was missing something. It didn't feel genuine. We used dried, pre-packaged noodles and our stocks were watered down with flavour enhancers. On the spur of the moment, I decided to fly to Tokyo. I would never become the next Jiro, that much I knew, but I wanted to be better, to do better, to lift our noodles to a higher level. In the end, that's what cooking is about: doing better every day. I had booked a hotel in Asakusa, a charming area near Ueno station. The daily Ameyoko open-air market occupies a long, narrow street beside the railway line. After the Second World War, this was the black market, full of American products; literally translated, the market is called "sweet street" (Ameya yokosho). Through a hole in the wall, I ordered **octopus balls** (takoyaki). These batter balls were very skilfully turned in a pan and, when ready, sprinkled with sweet Worcestershire sauce, Japanese mayonnaise and garnished with bonito flakes and green seaweed (aonori). In the evening, the market was taken down and the atmosphere was very different: the deafening noise from a pachinko arcade really did make me cross the street. I took up residence on a stool in a yakitori bar, serving roasted kebabs, and ordered a Sapporo beer and some kebabs with liver and shiitake. As a snack, I had **cucumber with spicy miso dip** (*morokyu*). I went entire days in search of hot bowls of ramen and I think I tried virtually every well-reviewed ramen shop in the Ueno neighbourhood.

I was *alone in Tokyo*, but I had a Belgian contact: a diplomat from Ghent who had lived there for years. Eric took me in tow to a crazy and colourful food-fest. When we found ourselves at a festival at the atmospheric Senso-ji temple and noticed some modern yatai, we bought something from all of them. From scoops of ice cream in a sandwich to grilled corn with miso. I'll never forget the comments from my companion, spoken in a broad Ghent accent. For example, when we saw blue and pink caramelised bananas hanging up, he was like, "Look, look, a blue banana!"

Now for something more serious. In Asakusa I discovered the Kappabashi Dori, an eight-hundred metre long shopping street that is a mecca for any chef. You can buy high-end kitchen appliances, razor-sharp knives and in fact everything the professional kitchen needs. In between all the noodle-slurping – I was eating ramen up to three times a day – I also hung around in Roppongi Hills, a very stylish building with great museums. The building provides a fabulous view across Tokyo and only then do you gain some idea of the true size of the city.
I discovered other districts, such as Ebisu, for myself and at breakneck speed. After years of travelling, I have developed a knack for scanning an area very quickly and then picking out only what interests me. I would not recommend that anyone follow me on such a trip because I really take it at an insane pace.

While in search of a ramen stand called Afuri, I came across Nakame-Guro, a most charming neighbourhood intersected by a canal, overhung with Japanese cherry trees. All of a sudden I was transported to Paris, with its little boutiques. I first had a **Japanese curry** (*yasai curry*) in Nakameguro, on the street, prepared and served from a caravan – real street food!

Every time I'm in Tokyo, I go to the world-renowned Tsukiji Fish Market in the mornings. I never get tired of looking and I can spend hours there. Every time it's the same ritual. I start every visit around 5 am by wandering around the fish auction. Then I take in the ambiance at the food carts around Shin-Ohashi-dori. I head for the market stalls for my first meal of the day. I order a beef stew or a steaming bowl of fatty ramen soup, washed down with a Kirin beer, I go to Rupan for coffee, then make a second trip to the nearby open-air market. This is true street food heaven. I order **miso soup with clams** (*asari no misoshiru*) or **fishcake with corn** (*toumorokushi no satsuma-age*) and, of course, **sushi**. There's no better place to order sushi. I have usually left by 11 o'clock: too many people!

So I went to Tokyo to research ramen, but as a bonus I learned an awful lot about street food and soon I had the idea of writing a book about it. For example, in Aoyama I came across Commune 246, a building full of food trucks and stands. The atmosphere was somewhat anarchistic, a little bit like Berlin, with a lot of vegan food as well as special hotdogs... I was surprised that such a thing existed in Tokyo!

A week and about twenty bowls of ramen soup later, I went back home, enriched with the taste of real ramen. Full of fresh motivation and inspiration, when I got home I immediately put the knowledge I had gained into practice. Since that trip to Tokyo, we now make the noodles and the stock at Ramen, our noodle bar, entirely ourselves – as it should be!

GOOD FOOD AND LOTS OF LAUGHTER

If Miho and I had to name our personal favourite event from 2016, it would undoubtedly be getting to know Tom and his colleagues at Eetavontuur, and Luk. That meeting, together with the culinary trip to Japan, enriched not only the entire year but also our lives.

We already knew of the existence of Eetavontuur and, out of curiosity, we had already been planning for some time to find out about potential collaboration. But we had never expected that we would collaborate so closely and intensely. Tom continues to energise us with his constant enthusiasm for the food culture. He is a "doer". Once he gets something into his head, he just "does" it, without delay or hanging about. Our travel experiences with him will remain a source of inspiration for our future activities. The atmosphere was always easy-going. But, at the same time, he kept an eye on what was important and he encouraged everyone to give their best. So we want to thank Tom for the wonderful opportunity. *Arigato*!

'Check it out!' seemed to be the perfect filler for Luk. 'Check it out!', and he showed us the photos he had just taken. We really enjoyed the photo ops. Sometimes Luk needed only a few seconds to identify an image, point the camera and take the photo. At other times, we would act as assistants and we created a shadow over a tiny little dish or held an automatic sliding door open. A few seconds after each photo was taken, we could look at it and we increasingly saw the book taking shape.

Our most important principle for life is "good food and lots of laughter". No matter how busy we are, even if we are almost falling over with fatigue, it doesn't matter: if we are together, there is laughter. So we don't mind a few laughter lines. After all, the Japanese saying goes: *Warau kado ni wa fuku kitaru*...or 'Fortune comes to those who laugh!'

Miho and I sometimes call each other 'my wife'. After Miho moved to Belgium, which is now more than ten years ago, we quickly became good friends, thanks to that shared philosophy of life, but also through our shared culinary interests. If we were to start something professionally involving Japanese cuisine, then it definitely had to be together. We are different, but in the positive sense of the word: we complement each other. Our catering business, Gohan, is therefore a typical example of *ninin sankyaku*, the game in which two people have to walk together with one leg attached to one of the other person's legs, as well as an expression that describes close collaboration.

In Japan we also say '*En ga aru*', which means having a kind of predestined bond. Without this 'en', this cookbook would have remained a pipedream. We already felt that 'bond' with each other and now we feel it with Tom and Luk too. As an example, when Miho started her first catering business with her husband, in 2005 they were featured in a magazine. The photographer who took their photograph at the time was – incredible but true – Luk Thys.

Tom and Luk understand each other to the core. Tom has a talent for finding great neighbourhoods with food stalls. He constantly surprised us and sometimes just disappeared. For instance, at the famous huge intersection in front of Shibuya station in Tokyo, he was sucked into the sea of people and seemed unreachable by phone. We were worried, but Luk calmly said, 'Relax, he'll be back.' And he just carried on taking photos of the city and, of course, after a while Tom just re-emerged from the same crowd.

To us, Street Food in Japan means primarily '*yatai*', of which I have an unforgettable memory. Soon after the major earthquake in Kobe in 1995, I was visiting friends in that largely devastated city. We went together to a huge yatai district that had appeared at lightning speed on a large piece of land where the wooden houses had been completely burned. Without a doubt, life was difficult for everyone there but the people looked lively and even happy because they could be together outside and could eat together. To my eyes, everywhere in Japan at that time looked chic and materialistic, so this showed me an entirely different (and forgotten) image. I felt then that the indefatigable Asian life force, which had been a mere slumbering presence in Japan, came to life again in this crisis. And I was proud of that.

CHICKEN KATSU チキンカツ
BREADED CHICKEN

Delicious with fresh coleslaw and sweet tonkatsu sauce

2 chicken fillets
2 eggs, lightly beaten
4 tablespoons flour
salt and pepper
100 g (⅔ cup) panko
tonkatsu sauce

Slice the chicken fillets lengthwise through the centre and pat dry thoroughly with paper towel. Lightly beat the eggs in a bowl. Put the flour into a separate bowl. Add a little salt and pepper. Put the panko into a third bowl.

Heat the cooking oil to 175 °C (350 °F). Coat the chicken slices in the flour, then in the lightly beaten egg and then press them firmly into the panko. Fry the breaded chicken for a few minutes until golden brown. Serve with tonkatsu sauce.

This works just as well with pork (tonkatsu).

ZARU SOBA ざるそば
ICE-COLD SOBA NOODLES WITH DIPPING SAUCE

This dish is often only available during the hot, humid summer season. "Zaru" means "reed sieve", since the noodles are served this way after being rinsed in cold water or with ice.

4 spring onions, cut into 4 cm (1 ½ inch) pieces, then julienned

3 cm (1 inch) ginger, peeled and grated

3 cm (1 inch) daikon, peeled and grated

1 teaspoon wasabi

1 teaspoon toasted white sesame seeds

Shichimi (Japanese seven-spice chile powder)

1 nori leaf, julienned

4 portions soba noodles

MENTSUYU

100 ml (½ cup) soy sauce

2 tablespoons mirin

1 ½ tablespoons sugar

200–400 ml (1–2 cups) dashi (see p. 196)

First make the mentsuyu. This is a mixture of kaeshi (soy sauce, mirin and sugar) and dashi. Heat the soy sauce with 2 tablespoons mirin and 1 ½ tablespoons sugar. Slowly bring to a boil until the alcohol has evaporated and it has all reduced slightly. Add the dashi to taste. Start with 200 ml (1 cup) and add more, depending on taste. You can keep this mixture in the refrigerator for two weeks.

Place the julienned spring onions in ice-cold water for 15 minutes, until they start to curl. Then drain completely. Put the ginger and the daikon on a square serving dish, together with the wasabi, spring onions, sesame seeds and the shichimi pepper. Very finely julienne half a nori leaf.

Boil the noodles according to the package directions. Then rinse in cold water or plunge into an ice bath. This removes all the surplus starch. Drain the noodles.

Serve the noodles on a bamboo or reed sieve or mat and sprinkle each portion with 1 tablespoon finely-chopped nori. Serve with a portion of mentsuyu dipping sauce and the dish of ginger, daikon, wasabi, sesame seeds and shichimi pepper. Dip the noodles with the seasoning into the mentsuyu sauce.

For a 100% vegetarian alternative, replace the dashi with shiitake stock.

Instead of shichimi, you can use ichimi, which is pure chile powder, without the other spices that are in shichimi.

OWARIYA
ASAKUSA 1-7-1, TAITO-KU
TOKIO 111-0032
OPEN: 11.30 AM – 8.30 PM

TAKOYAKI たこ焼き
OCTOPUS BALLS

This is the first street food snack I came across in Japan. Watching it being made is an amazing sight.

250 g (2 cups) flour

2 teaspoons baking powder

½ teaspoon salt

2 eggs

350 ml (1 ½ cups) dashi (see p. 196)

1 teaspoon soy sauce

peanut oil

100 g (4 ounces) octopus, cooked and cut into pieces

2 spring onions, in thin rings

¼ cup panko

1 tablespoon pickled pink ginger, in strips

1 tablespoon dashi powder

Japanese mayonnaise

tonkatsu sauce (see p. 203)

1 tablespoon dried green seaweed powder (aonori)

¼ cup bonito flakes (katsuobushi), ground to powder with a pestle and mortar

Put the flour in a mixing bowl and add the baking powder and salt. Beat the eggs lightly and add to the bowl. Mix in the dashi and soy sauce. You must create a smooth batter, a bit like pancake batter. Pour the batter into a jug.

Heat the takoyaki pan. Coat with peanut oil. As soon as the pan starts to smoke, pour the batter from the jug into the holes. Place a small amount of octopus, spring onion, panko and pickled ginger on each portion of batter. Top with a little dashi powder.

Fry a little, but not completely. The batter must still be runny on the inside. Now carefully turn the balls over in the pan. The batter that is still runny will form the base of the balls. Fry for a further 4 minutes and turn the balls over again a couple of times. Remove the balls from the pan. Place on a plate. Garnish with mayonnaise, tonkatsu sauce, green seaweed and bonito flakes.

MARKET STREET

GANKOTAKO
MEGURO 3-11-6, MEGURO-KU
TOKIO 153-0063
OPEN DAILY: 11 AM – 1 AM

HANADAKO
KAKUDA-CHO 9-16, KITA-KU
OSAKA 530-0017
OPEN DAILY: 10 AM – 11 PM

MISO 味噌

My grandparents' house in Hiroshima had a huge store room with wooden sliding doors. Inside the store room there was always a large porcelain pitcher of miso that my grandmother had made.

The house was originally built as a tea house, so it had two rooms that were intended for the tea ceremony, one on the ground floor and another on the first floor, both with a *rodan* (sunken hearth) and a low *shoji* (sliding door with wooden frame, across which white paper is stretched). The garden was also very Japanese, with large ornamental stones and beautifully trimmed trees. In order to go to the toilet, I had to use an exterior corridor, which bordered the garden with its lovely view. In the evenings, it was very scary. When it was dark, I did not dare look into the garden. My grandmother taught *ikebana* (flower arranging) at home and my grandfather's hobby was growing bonsai and vegetables.

When I think about the taste and smell of my grandmother's miso, all these things merge in my mind and make me quite nostalgic. When I was a child, I was amazed at how the colour of the miso changed from pale to dark over the month-long process. Now I know that the miso was in fact "alive".

It is a known fact that miso is made from soy beans but in the West it is perhaps not as well known that there are different varieties. To start with, there are three types of *koji* fungus (yeast): rice koji, wheat koji and soy koji. They also vary in taste, from salty to sweet. The taste is determined primarily by the amount of salt, but also by the amount of koji fungus. The more koji is added, the sweeter the flavour. Previously, miso was also used inland – where there was no sea – as a means of storing salt. Then there are also different shades of colour. When the amino acid in soy beans reacts with sugar, the colour becomes darker.

Miso originally came from China, about thirteen hundred years ago, so it has a long history in Japan. Today, miso soup is well-known all over the world but miso only became popular as a soup from the twelfth century onwards, as part of a plain but healthy meal. Nowadays, miso can be prepared in many ways, including as a marinade for fish and meat, *tare* (dipping sauce) or vinaigrette. It is used every day in Japanese cuisine and increasingly in Western cooking.

MOROKYU もろきゅう
CUCUMBER WITH SPICY MISO DIP

4 cucumbers

2 tablespoons white miso paste

1 tablespoon mirin

1 teaspoon chile oil

Slice the cucumber lengthwise into six pieces and remove the seeds. If you prefer smaller pieces, you can cut it again into 4-cm (2-inch) long sticks.

Mix the miso with the mirin and the chile oil. Serve the cucumber on a dish with the miso dip.

IZAKAYA

STANDING BAR

YASAI CURRY 野菜カレー
JAPANESE CURRY WITH VEGETABLES

Curry shops are everywhere in Japan!

2 tablespoons peanut oil

2 onions, coarsely chopped

3 potatoes, in 2-cm (1-inch) chunks

2 carrots, in 1-cm (½-inch) chunks

750 ml (3 cups) water

150 g (5 ounces) Japanese curry cubes

1 tablespoon soy sauce

Put 2 tablespoons of peanut oil in a large saucepan. Add the onion and fry over low heat. Add the potatoes and the carrots. Cover with water and bring slowly to the boil. Dissolve the curry cubes in the water. Finish with soy sauce.

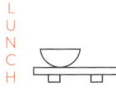

ASARI NO MISOSHIRU
あさりの味噌汁
MISO SOUP WITH CLAMS

During spring and summer in Japan, "hunting" for clams is a popular activity. Japanese people head for the coast at this time and, at low tide, they scoop clams out of the sand and collect them. Back at home, the first meal that Miho's father always made was miso soup with the freshly-collected clams. So, for her, the strong, pure taste of that miso soup with fresh clams is still one of the best meals ever.

500 g (1 pound) clams

800 ml (4 cups) dashi (see p. 196)

2 to 4 tablespoons miso

a handful of spring onions, finely chopped in rings

To remove sand, place the clams in salt water for 3 hours (500 ml (1 pint) water with 1 tablespoon salt). The shells will then open and expel the sand. Then rinse the clams another 3 times in salt water.

Bring the dashi to the boil. Put the miso in a deep ladle and place it just into the soup. Stirring constantly with chopsticks, dissolve the miso in the spoon. Stir the dissolved miso gradually into the soup so as not to create any lumps.

Drain the clams and add to the boiling stock. Turn off the heat when the shells open. Distribute them among the serving dishes and garnish with spring onion.

If clams are not available, other shellfish can be used, such as cockles or scallops, etc.

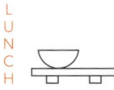

TOMOROKOSHI NO SATSUMA-AGE
とうもろこしのさつま揚げ
FISHCAKE WITH CORN

A basic fishcake is traditionally eaten just with soy sauce, but you can also stir-fry it in a wok or boil it in stock. In this dish, the basic fishcake is combined with corn. Not only does this make it more attractive in terms of colour and shape, but it also combines sweet and sour to create a more complex flavour. This is Tomoko's favourite dish!

300 g (10 ounces) cod, skinless and boneless

1 egg

½ teaspoon salt

a pinch of sugar

1 tablespoon sake

2 tablespoons potato starch

2 teaspoons ginger, grated

300 g (10 ounces) corn niblets

Place all the ingredients except the corn niblets into the blender and blend into a smooth fish paste. Shape the paste into a disc 1 cm (½ inch) thick and 4 cm (1 ½ inches) in diameter. Cover the disc entirely with corn niblets. Heat the frying oil to 160 °C (320 °F) and fry it for 4 to 5 minutes. Drain on paper towel and serve with soy sauce, if desired.

To make a basic fishcake, just omit the corn from this recipe. It will be just as delicious!

IZAKAYA

MARKET STREET

NIGIRI SUSHI にぎり寿司
SUSHI BALLS TOPPED WITH FISH

You need years of experience to make good sushi. A true sushi master is akin to an artist. We all love watching as he makes a rice ball in one swift movement and immediately tops it with fish. This recipe is an easy version in which you make the rice balls first and then place the fish on top. Try not to make the rice balls or the fish too big, so that the pieces can be eaten in one bite.

500 g (1 pound) fresh fish fillet (salmon, tuna, scallops, bass, etc.)

6 small bowls sushi rice (see p. 199)

soy sauce

wasabi

Cut the fish fillet into slices approximately 5 mm (¼ inch) thick, 3 cm x 5 cm (1 x 2 inches). Store them in the refrigerator. Wet your hands and shape the rice into oval balls, approximately 2 cm x 3 cm (1 x 1.5 inches) and 1.5 cm (¾ inch) high. Take a rice ball in your left hand and place a slice of fish on it. Push down on the fish with the index and middle fingers of your right hand. Place the sushi on a plate and serve with soy sauce and wasabi.

Sushi rolls wrapped in nori leaves are known as gunkan-sushi. You can fill these with small pieces of fish, salmon roe, cucumber, etc..

IZAKAYA IN KYOTO

More than ten years after my first Japanese experience – and much culinary knowledge the wiser – I landed with my current girlfriend, Sandra, at Kansai Airport. This time, my destination was Kyoto, right in the middle of cherry blossom season, which is definitely the most beautiful and most romantic time to visit Kyoto. Kyoto receives over thirty million visitors per year and has seventeen sites recognised by UNESCO. The city is well known for its pickles – an essential aspect of Japanese cuisine – which are used in virtually every meal. The star of the culinary line-up in Kyoto is *kaiseki* (haute cuisine): a traditional meal consisting of a number of courses following a fixed order and in which a great deal of attention is devoted to presentation, texture, colour and variety.

For a thousand years, Kyoto was the capital so, from a cultural perspective, it is truly unmissable. We rented bicycles to travel around the city and there can be no better way to start a bike ride than with lunch. At Kyoto station we ordered a portion of **tantan ramen** (*tantanmen*), then Sandra and I cycled through the Nishiki Market. At the food carts, we sampled the different kinds of **pickles** for which Kyoto is famous. We bought a couple of **thick pancakes filled with sweetened adzuki beans** (*dorayaki*) and ate them on a bench in the beautiful imperial garden in the heart of Kyoto. We were familiar with this dessert from the Japanese film *An* (released in English as *Sweet Bean*), about an older lady who makes the filling for these "buns".

We also took bike rides to the major attractions, such as the Arashiyama districts and the Philosopher's Walk, which starts at the Silver Pagoda. On this Philosopher's Walk – a tree-lined path along the water – you can actually see wise men walking. I don't have green fingers but I love Japanese gardens. For me, a little walking, a little contemplation, a stop at one of the tea houses on the way and ordering a green tea – that is ultimate peace.

We strolled on foot through Gion, Kyoto's legendary geisha district. They do still exist: girls who are raised to be geishas, escorts who have to learn particular manners and rituals. The geishas live in the district with a kind of "geisha mother" and if you are lucky you'll see them on the street on the way to a rendezvous, traditionally dressed and made up.

Entirely in keeping with the tone of our romantic holiday, we discovered an amazing spot during this trip. It's called Wife and Husband and it's a tiny coffee bar run by a couple – and it's typically Japanese! You push open the little door and suddenly you're in an entirely different world. The Japanese have a natural talent for design, style, interior decor and atmosphere. It's one surprise after another.

The Japanese are also highly disciplined. But after work, around five in the afternoon, you see a very different side of Japan in the *izakayas* or Japanese pubs. After their daily grind, people (especially men) go down to an *izakaya* for a beer or a sake, as well as for a snack. There are different levels of izakaya, from very smoky, pub-like places to chic establishments. But the idea is always the same: you sit at the bar or in groups of six at booths, you share small plates and you drink. Snacks are tapas-style, but more refined and varied. Entirely by accident, Sandra and I ended up in virtually the best *izakaya* in Kyoto – maybe because it was our first time. Its owner was so proud that we – two Belgians – were at his place, that he really pampered us. The chef showed us a lovely piece of vacu-

um-packed beef, barely 300 grams (10 ounces) I'd estimate, with very thick white nerves in it. Before we even noticed, that slice of meat was on a plate under our noses, in thick slices and perfectly grilled. A little soy sauce, coarse sea salt, wasabi and a wedge of lemon were served on the side. It was wagyu beef from Miyasaki. I had never tasted such delicious meat. I often think back with nostalgia about that when I order meat at a Belgian restaurant.

What followed was a finger-licking culinary journey: **marinated bamboo shoots** (menma), **marinated and fried chicken** (tori no karaage), delicious **grilled scallops with soy sauce and butter** (hotate no grill) and **grilled aubergine with bonito flakes** (yaki nasu) and **tofu balls in a thick dashi sauce** (Tofu-dango no ankake). It went on for the whole evening. Drinking buddies on both sides showed us their food, gave us recommendations and treated us to snacks. The discovery of the izakaya concept and very specifically of this particular eatery was a highlight of our trip. The hospitality, the friendliness and the culinary orgasm combined to produce an unforgettable experience!

TANTANMEN 担担麺
RAMEN WITH SPICY MINCED MEAT

Spicy tantan ramen is one of Tom's personal favourites. This dish has now become a fixture at his noodle bar in Ghent.

200 g (8 ounces) mixed minced meat (beef/pork)

2 tablespoons vegetable oil

2 cm (1 inch) ginger, finely minced

1 spring onion

1 clove garlic, finely minced

1 tablespoon tobanjan paste

240 ml (1 cup) chicken stock (see p. 200)

240 ml (1 cup) dashi (see p. 196)

2 portions ramen noodles

2 tablespoons tantandare (see p. 204)

1 tablespoon chicken fat

1 tablespoon pork fat

½ teaspoon kastuobushi salt (see p. 199)

10 g hare's ear mushrooms, soaked, hard parts removed

1 soft-boiled egg

2 spring onions, julienned

a few nori leaves, 8 x 4 cm (3 x 1.5 inches)

Heat the oil and fry the spring onion and ginger over a low heat. Add the minced meat. Stir-fry the minced meat and add the tobanjan paste. Set aside.

Heat the chicken stock with the dashi in a saucepan.

Boil the noodles in water until cooked.

Put the tantandare into a noodle bowl, add the fat and the katsuobushi salt. Pour a small amount of the chicken-dashi over them, so that the fat "melts" a little. Add the noodles and place the minced meat on them. Sprinkle some hare's ear mushrooms to one side of the noodles, place half an egg on the other side. Pour the stock over everything. Garnish with the spring onion strips and stand a nori leaf beside the stock. Repeat this for the second portion. Serve as hot as possible.

HAKUSAI NO TSUKEMONO
白菜の漬物
PICKLED CHINESE CABBAGE

In Japan, this is usually eaten with white rice, but it can also be a snack, with a cup of sake for example. You can make this dish with very simple ingredients but it's the kombu that gives it its unique umami flavour.

3 g kombu (seaweed), 1% of the weight of the cabbage

9 g (3/10 ounce) coarse salt, 3% of the weight of the cabbage

300 g (10 ounces) Chinese cabbage

1 dried red chile pepper

Carefully weigh the correct amount of salt and seaweed. The weight ratio of the vegetables and the spices is very important. Cut the kombu with scissors into thin strips, approximately 3 mm x 2 cm (⅛ inch x 1 inch). Rinse the Chinese cabbage in water and drain well. Cut the cabbage into pieces approximately 10 cm (4 inches) long and place in a freezer bag. Add salt and seaweed and mix well. Then add the hot chile pepper. Squeeze as much of the air out of the bag as possible and seal it. Store the cabbage for at least 12 hours in the refrigerator. Turn the bag occasionally so that the marinade is redistributed.

When the cabbage has released enough water, it is ready. Cut the cabbage into smaller pieces and serve.

You can also marinate other vegetables, such as daikon leaves (white Spanish radish), the daikon itself, carrot, cucumber, etc.. A small piece of yuzu peel imparts an extra fresh flavour.

DORAYAKI どら焼き
THICK PANCAKES WITH SWEETENED ADZUKI BEANS

Dorayaki is the favourite food of Doraemon, one of the best-known Japanese anime characters, as well as Tomoko's and her father's favourite. A girlfriend of mine once baked an enormous dorayaki for her birthday and literally "filled" it with affection. In the film *An* (2015), by Naomi Kawase, you can see how far dedication to this one food can go!

2 eggs
50 g (¼ cup) sugar
50 ml (¼ cup) milk
2 teaspoons mirin
100 g (1 cup) flour, sifted
1 teaspoon baking powder
250 g (8 ounces) sweetened adzuki beans (see p. 206)

Beat eggs, sugar, milk and mirin in a bowl. Add flour and baking powder and mix well. Leave to stand for 15 minutes in the refrigerator.

Spread a layer of oil in the frying pan using paper towel and place on the heat. Using a soup spoon, pour the batter into the frying pan and make pancakes 6 cm (2 ½ inches) in diameter. Fry uncovered. Flip the pancakes when the batter starts to bubble and fry until light brown.

Place the pancakes on a plate and leave to cool. Place adzuki beans on half of the pancakes and then cover with the remaining pancakes. Serve at room temperature.

MARKET STREET

24/7

TORI NO KARAAGE 鶏の唐揚げ
MARINATED AND FRIED CHICKEN

This is one of almost everyone's favourite dishes. It can be found everywhere – from bento boxes to izakaya restaurants and from party meals to comfort food at home. This recipe is of course at its most delicious when freshly made but the meat remains tender when it has cooled. As a result, leftovers are usually used in lunch boxes the next day.

600 g (1 ¼ pounds) chicken leg fillets (skinless, boneless)

4 tablespoons potato starch

MARINADE

2 teaspoons grated garlic

2 teaspoons grated ginger

1 teaspoon sugar

1 teaspoon salt

4 tablespoons potato starch

1 egg

1 tablespoon soy sauce

2 tablespoons sesame oil

⅓ teaspoon Szechuan pepper

Combine all the marinade ingredients in a bowl. Cut the chicken into approximately 3 x 4 cm (1 x 1.5 inch) chunks. Use your hands to mix the marinade with the chicken and massage the marinade into the meat. Cover and place in the refrigerator for at least 1 hour.

Remove the chicken from the refrigerator and sprinkle the potato starch over the meat. Heat the oil to 180 °C (350 °F) and fry the chicken until golden brown. Drain the meat on a paper towel and serve.

LUNCH

IZAKAYA

STANDING BAR

24/7

HOTATE NO GRILL
ホタテのバター醤油
GRILLED SCALLOPS WITH SOY SAUCE AND BUTTER

Delicious, tasty scallops are found on Japan's most northerly island, Hokkaido, which also boasts very good butter. This dish is the perfect izakaya snack.

4 scallops, with shell
4 teaspoons butter
2 teaspoons soy sauce
¼ teaspoon salt

Open the scallops with an oyster knife. Remove the scallop, together with the black part (stomach) and the liver. Set the scallop aside. Rinse the shell under running water to remove any sand. Place the scallop back on the shell and place the shell over a charcoal fire. Place 1 teaspoon of butter on each scallop and add ½ teaspoon of soy sauce. Grill for 2 minutes and turn the scallop on the shell. Sprinkle with a pinch of salt and serve.

You can also make this dish without the shells. In that case, fry the scallops in the pan until almost ready, then melt a small pat of butter over them at the end, garnish with the soy sauce.

TOFU-DANGO NO ANKAKE
TOFU BALLS WITH THICK DASHI SAUCE

YAKI NASU
**GRILLED AUBERGINE WITH BONITO FLAKES
SEE P. 60**

TOFU-DANGO NO ANKAKE
豆腐団子のあんかけ
TOFU BALLS WITH THICK DASHI SAUCE

In Japan, tofu is often mixed with minced meat so that you are also including healthy plant protein with the meat. The combination with the thick sauce is delicious. The advantage of this thick sauce is that it retains the heat of the dish for longer.

BALLS

250 g (8 ounces) momen tofu (firm tofu)

5 cm (2 inches) carrot, in small chunks

200 g (7 ounces) minced chicken

4 scampi, peeled, in 1-cm (½ inch) pieces

10 cm (4 inches) spring onion, in thin rings

⅓ teaspoon salt

1 tablespoon sake

1 teaspoon juice of grated ginger

2 tablespoons potato starch

SAUCE

1 ½ tablespoons soy sauce

1 ½ tablespoons mirin

150 ml (⅔ cup) dashi (see p. 196)

1 tablespoon potato starch

Wrap the tofu in paper towel and place on a microwave-safe plate. Heat for 5 minutes in the microwave at 600 W, uncovered. Heat the carrots for 2 minutes in the microwave at 600 W, covered. Put all the ingredients for the balls in a bowl and mix with your hands. Make six balls from the mixture.

Place a piece of microwave-safe film, approximately 30 x 30 cm (12 x 12 inches) on the work surface. Place a ball in the centre of the film. Bring the four corners of the film together and twist the film as tightly as possible. Repeat this procedure for each of the balls. Place the six balls on a flat plate with the corners of the film upwards. Unwind the film very slightly so that the ball does not explode when heated. Heat for 5 minutes in the microwave at 600 W.

Put all the sauce ingredients in a saucepan and mix well using a whisk. Bring slowly to the boil. Stir regularly until the sauce has thickened.

Remove the balls from the film and place them on a plate. Spoon the sauce over them and serve.

You can also use minced pork instead of minced chicken.

MARKET STREET

YAKI NASU 焼きナス
GRILLED AUBERGINE WITH BONITO FLAKES

A very simple dish; the combination of bonito flakes, ginger and a little soy sauce is to die for!

1 thick aubergine, approximately 8-9 cm (3-3 ½ inches) in diameter

1 teaspoon ginger, grated

half a handful bonito flakes

soy sauce to taste

Remove the top of the aubergine and score it lengthwise to make it easier to peel later. Grill the whole aubergine in the oven until the skin turns black. Turn the aubergine until it is black all over.

Leave the aubergine to cool and peel by hand from top to bottom. Divide the aubergine into four pieces, place on a plate and garnish with grated ginger, bonito flakes and soy sauce to taste.

You can also grill the aubergine on the barbecue. Do not forget to cut off the top or to score the aubergine, otherwise it will "explode".

TEAM-BUILDING JAPAN

Five fellow chefs who set off for eighteen days in search of inspiring dishes, take the craziest train journeys in order to discover and to consume as much food as possible. Think of breakfasts on trains and in convenience stores, lunches in restaurants and then in the evenings going on a food crawl through cities – all at an insane pace. Time out from our kitchen as well as from all the associated stress: that was the idea behind my most recent trip to Japan, which I took in the autumn of 2016 with four colleagues: Pieterjan, Benoit, Ciska and Laurens. I think we took around sixty train rides, all using the Japan Rail Pass, which allows you to travel freely around the vastly extensive Japan Rail network. I think that throughout the entire trip, we went out to eat about four or five times per day, always casually: as cheap and easily accessible as possible. So it was a crazy food expedition, with room on all sides for tourist visits.

Our itinerary included Fukuoka plus side trips and Osaka plus side trips. Afterwards, the team was to fly home and I would stay a little longer in order to take another food expedition to Tokyo, this time accompanied by Tomoko and Miho.

It was still very early when we landed in Osaka; nothing in the city was open yet. So our food expedition started as soon as we landed. Almost everywhere in Japan you can find convenience stores along the lines of 7-Eleven, FamilyMart and Lawson's, all of them offering a "world of snacks". So as soon as we arrived, we ordered *onigiri* – at one euro per piece. Freshly made every day, a choice of ten varieties, and we had our first snack! We ordered triangular white crustless sandwiches with egg, ham and cheese, also found in Italy and known there as *tramezzino*. The sandwiches melted in our mouths. The **triangular breaded chicken sandwich** (*chicken katsu sando*) was also very tasty. For the rest of our trip, we would get breakfast from these convenience stores. They were a real discovery!

A JR pass provides such freedom to travel that you really do take the train to wherever you can. Right after those first snacks, we made tracks. Our ultimate goal for that day was Fukuoka, a three-hour journey, but our first stop was Okayama. There, we had the most delicious tofu of our lives. We pushed open a small sliding door and bumped into a curtain: cautiously, we poked our heads around and peeked inside. A friendly lady showed us to a spot at the bar and welcomed us with a warm *dozo* (you're welcome). She told us how she makes fresh tofu every day and took us through to her little traditional factory behind the shop. She continued to explain about the cooking process – all in Japanese! We nodded *hai* (yes) and *arigato* (thank you) to be polite and acted as if we fully understood her Japanese explanation.

If you think that tofu just tastes dull, here is a good comparison. There's the mozzarella that you can buy at your local supermarket and then there's the genuine Italian *burrata*. So, the tofu there at the tofu shop was the burrata experience. We also ordered **vegetables with "broken" tofu** (*yasai no shiraae*), **rice bowl with yuba and thick dashi sauce** (*yuba no donburi*) and **cold tofu with various types of garnish and soy sauce** (*hiyayakko*).

We strolled through Korakuen, the Japanese gardens of Okayama – a very peaceful place to wander! Just outside the garden, we got talking

to the chef of the restaurant, a very fine young man who had just become a father. He told us how he used to travel around as a backpacker and how he was already looking forward to the time when he could again travel the world... His restaurant was located on a platform on the banks of a lake, with a view of Okayama castle. What a spectacular setting: wooden chairs and tables, with a perfect balance between the interior and its surroundings. There, we ate freshly-made **udon noodles with oysters** (kake udon) and udon noodles with fried vegetables (yasai no kakiage udon). The oysters came from Hiroshima and tasted wonderful. The noodles were cooked between al dente and soft. Nothing beats fresh, home-made and hand-pulled udon noodles. The vegetables were cooked to perfection and fried until crispy. Everyone had their noodles and everyone was happy! But most of all – boom! – everyone was right in the heart of Japan.

CHICKEN KATSU SANDO
チキンカツサンド
TRIANGULAR BREADED CHICKEN SANDWICH

One of Tom's favourite morning bites.

juice of 1 lemon
2 tablespoons olive oil
½ teaspoon salt
16 slices white bread, crusts removed
Japanese mayonnaise
½ cucumber, sliced
8 tablespoons tonkatsu sauce (see p. 203)
⅛ white cabbage, finely shredded
8 pieces breaded chicken, chicken katsu (see p. 27)

First make the coleslaw. Add the lemon juice, olive oil and salt to the cabbage and mix well.

Cut the white bread into triangles. Arrange them in sets of two. Spread one side with mayonnaise and cover with cucumber. Spread the other side with the tonkatsu sauce and cover with coleslaw. Place the chicken on top and sandwich together.

YASAI NO SHIRAAE 野菜の白和え
VEGETABLES WITH "BROKEN" TOFU

Broken tofu gives the vegetables a mild flavour. Combined with the toasted sesame seeds, this is a rich vegetarian dish.

250 g (9 ounces) momen tofu (firm tofu)

5 cm (2 inches) carrot, in thin strips

200 g (8 ounces) spinach

3 tablespoons toasted sesame seeds

4 tablespoons sugar

2 tablespoons soy sauce

Wrap the tofu in paper towel and place on a microwave-safe dish. Heat for 5 minutes in the microwave at 600 W, uncovered. Place the carrots on a microwave-safe dish with a lid and heat for 2 minutes in the microwave at 600 W. Blanch the spinach for a few seconds in boiling salted water and drain. Cool in iced water and then squeeze out the moisture. Toast the sesame seeds in a pan without oil until they smell good. Pour the sesame seeds into the bowl of a food mixer while they are still hot. Grind the seeds briefly but do not turn them into powder. Put the tofu in a bowl and mash with a fork. Add sesame seeds, sugar and soy sauce and mix well. Mix the vegetables with the tofu paste and serve.

You can use other vegetables too. Persimmon (finely chopped without boiling) is also ideally suited for this type of preparation.

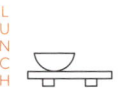

OKABE
OMOTE-CHO 1-10-1, KITA-KU
OKAYAMA 700-0822
OPEN: MON-WEDS/FRI-SAT, 11.30 AM – 2 PM

YASAI NO SHIRAAE
VEGETABLES WITH "BROKEN" TOFU

HIYAYAKKO
**COLD TOFU WITH VARIOUS TYPES OF GARNISH AND SOY SAUCE
SEE P. 70**

YUBA NO DONBURI
DON (RICE BOWL) WITH YUBA AND THICK DASHI SAUCE

YASAI NO SHIRAAE
VEGETABLES WITH "BROKEN" TOFU SEE P. 66

YUBA NO DONBURI 湯葉のどんぶり
DON (RICE BOWL) WITH YUBA AND THICK DASHI SAUCE

Yuba is a thin skin that is produced when you boil soy milk. It feels wonderful in your mouth. Dried yuba is easier to obtain. Japanese monks who had studied in China introduced yuba in the thirteenth century as a vegetarian ingredient of meals in Zen temples. Yuba is also used in soup, as a garnish for sushi and for rolling up various ingredients.

900 ml (1 quart) dashi (see p. 196)

2 tablespoons sugar

1 tablespoon sake

3 tablespoons mirin

120 g (4 ounces) dried yuba leaves (dried soy milk skin)

4 small bowls cooked rice (see p. 198)

3 tablespoons soy sauce

1 teaspoon salt

ground Szechuan pepper to taste (optional)

3 tablespoons potato starch

3 tablespoons water

nori leaves, cut into strips

Mix the dashi, sugar, sake and mirin in a pan and bring to the boil. Add the dried yuba leaves and cook for another 3 to 4 minutes over a low heat until the yuba leaves soften. Scoop some hot rice into each bowl. Strain off the yuba leaves but reserve the cooking liquid. Place the yuba leaves on the rice.

Add soy sauce, salt and ground Szechuan pepper, if using, to the cooking liquid and boil for 1 minute. Remove the sauce from the heat. Put the potato starch and water into a bowl and mix well. Add the mixture to the sauce and stir until the sauce has thickened. Return the sauce to the heat and bring to boiling point. Remove the sauce from the heat. Spoon it over the yuba leaves and serve with nori strips.

OKABE
OMOTE-CHO 1-10-1, KITA-KU
OKAYAMA 700-0822
OPEN: MON-WEDS/
FRI-SAT, 11.30 AM – 2 PM

HIYAYAKKO 冷奴
COLD TOFU WITH VARIOUS TYPES OF GARNISH AND SOY SAUCE

This is a very simple, healthy, low-calorie and popular dish in Japan. The flavourful garnish (fresh ginger, spring onion, bonito and soy sauce) even wins over those who usually don't like tofu. So give it a try!

1 packet tofu (soft tofu, e.g. silken)

1 teaspoon ginger, grated

1 tablespoon spring onion, in thin rings

half a handful bonito flakes

soy sauce

Open the tofu packet carefully so as not to break up the tofu and place it on a plate. Cut into six or eight pieces. Garnish the tofu with ginger, spring onion and bonito flakes. Pour soy sauce over the tofu to taste and serve.

You can garnish this simple dish with other ingredients, such as finely chopped sashimi with wasabi or thinly sliced cooked meat with miso sauce.

STANDING BAR

LUNCH

OKABE
OMOTE-CHO 1-10-1, KITA-KU
OKAYAMA 700-0822
OPEN: MON-WEDS/FRI-SAT, 11.30 AM – 2 PM

KAKI UDON
牡蠣うどん

UDON NOODLES WITH OYSTERS

Udon are thick, white noodles often served in a warm dashi stock. You will find many standing bars in or near stations, selling these (or other) noodles.

80 g dried udon noodles

12 to 16 oysters without shells

5 cm (2 inches) daikon (white Spanish radish), grated

1.4 l (1 ½ quarts) dashi (see p. 196)

6 tablespoons soy sauce

½ tablespoon mirin

½ tablespoon sugar

spring onions, finely sliced

Cook the udon according to the package directions. Wash the noodles immediately in cold water once they are cooked so as to stop the cooking process. Drain in a colander. Place the oysters in a large bowl and add the grated daikon. Use the daikon as soap and wash the oysters very carefully by hand. The daikon will turn grey from the sand and dirt from the oysters. Rinse the oysters in cold water without breaking them. Place the dashi, soy sauce, mirin and sugar in a pan and bring to the boil. Add the oysters to the boiling stock and remove them from the liquid as soon as they are cooked. Pour the udon noodles and the spring onions into the boiling stock to heat them up and turn off the heat. Distribute into four bowls and serve immediately.

You can use soba noodles (thin buckwheat noodles) instead of udon noodles (thick wheat noodles). In Japanese restaurants, you can always choose between udon and soba noodles for dashi. If you put tempura on top instead of noodles, that makes tempura udon.

KORAKUEN
INGANG ZUID, KORAKUEN 1-5,
KITA-KU, OKAYAMA 703-8257
OPEN DAILY: 10 AM – 6 PM

FUKUOKA – THE HOME OF TONKOTSU

I had booked a ryokan in advance, so we could sleep Japanese-style right from the start. A *ryokan* is typically Japanese accommodation that usually also has a spa. I really love Japanese bathing culture. It was a fairly old ryokan, but perfect in terms of atmosphere, all wood, sliding doors, tatami, futon, etc.. You put on your slippers and *yukata* (a robe a bit like a kimono) and head for the spa. It's an ideal way to recover from travelling. Here's one amusing detail: Ciska wasn't paying attention and she immediately washed in the public bath, rather than using the taps provided for that purpose in the bathroom.

Once we had washed and rested, we went straight into the city in search of *yatai*, or Japanese food carts. Fukuoka is the epicentre of the *yatai* culture, with around 150 *yatai*. To be honest, our first encounter with *yatai* in Tenjin, a neighbourhood of Fukuoka, did not go smoothly. There were five of us but apparently you could only sit around this type of cart in a group of between six and eight. When we arrived at around eight in the evening, everything was already full. So we decided to split up: Benoit, Ciska and Pieterjan sat down at a yatai stand, while Laurens and I went into a *kushikatsu* bar. We ordered a variety of **deep-fried skewered meat and vegetables** (*kushikatsu*). There was a dipping sauce on the counter with a sign beside it saying you may only dip once, which is logical from a hygiene perspective. But they are very strict about it – *you only dip once!* – or you're thrown out. They also serve cabbage with it, so if you want sauce a second time, you can dip using a piece of cabbage.

We went to find our travelling companions again and together we set off on an extreme food expedition. We sampled one thing after another in alleys, narrow streets and neighbourhoods. I remember livers and balls of batter with sesame seed, but especially the **deep-fried skewered chicken** (*yakitori*) that I ordered in a small restaurant called Kawaya. There was no holding us back; on the way home, we even stopped by a yatai. Something was simmering in a large pot: **daikon, egg and fishcake in stock** (*oden*). I ordered that, somewhat intrigued by what I had read about oden, and my portion was served with... mustard! Daikon, simmered for hours in a dashi stock, with **mustard** of all things. I thought, I'm eating *hutsepot* (a type of Belgian stew) But it was a real hit – a primal taste memory and pure soul food.

The next day, Laurens, Benoit and I woke up fairly early, while Ciska and Pieterjan were still sleeping. The three of us decided to go in search of the genuine **ramen with pork stock** (*tonkotsu ramen*). Laurens could not take the penetrating odour of pork stock so early in the morning so on the way he ate an **omelette on fried rice** (*omuraisu*), but Benoit and I went for the full-on **pork stock** (*tonkotsu*) experience. We then found an amazing place at the Fukuoka fish market. The place was open day and night, taxi drivers ate there, workers ordered their breakfast there, etc.. The soup was seriously delicious, and very plain – stock, noodles and **marinated braised pork** (*chashu*) – but a pure explosion of flavour.

Later, we sneaked into the fish market – literally. That type of fish market is not really open to the general public, but we got in anyway. This type of market always has a section with a couple of sushi restaurants. There, we ate **sashimi on rice bowl** (kaisen don), one of the revelations of our trip. The dish consists of rice that is still warm, with some perilla leaves – large shiso leaves – on top, then fish sashimi is placed on top of that and everything is garnished with herbs, some soy sauce and some wasabi.... We had a great meal for only 4.5 euros, or 500 yen! And that included sliced fresh mackerel. Perfect rice, perfect fish! This was something entirely new to me, plus of course there was also the secrecy aspect of, "We're not really supposed to be here". The naughty boys who had cleverly managed to sneak inside. Sometimes, you just need to have some guts.

We met the other half of our team at the Muji Store and the five of us took a walk to the sea and Fukuoka Tower – but not without the compulsory food stop of course. At the deli in a shopping arcade we bought **sardines with ginger** (iwashi no nitsuke), **spinach with sesame sauce** (horenso no gomaae) and **potato salad** (poteto salada) – not something usually associated with Japan, but nonetheless very popular.

Our second yatai attempt in another part of town was an immediate success. By that time, we had become wiser; we were ready even before the yatai carts were set up. One by one, they were towed in by motorcycle, empty beer crates were stacked and placed on top of each other to use as chairs, plastic curtains were hung around the carts for protection and the fires were lit for grilling. You could really sense the atmosphere of the impending culinary feast.

Once we sat down, we ate and drank abundantly. One friendly owner explained each of her dishes. What stuck with me the most is the local speciality, **cod roe tempura with perilla leaves** (mentaiko to shiso no tempura): crispy-fried tempura, the fresh perilla leaf, the soft texture and the salty taste of the roe – what an explosion of taste!

And to finish off our Fukuoka food tour? What do you think? More ramen, but something completely different from the conventional tonkotsu. Half of our group jumped at **pesto ramen** (basil ramen). It was a blast! The basil perfectly complemented the pork. The other boys went for **dipping noodles** (tsukemen) in a hut by the door. Dipping noodles. That is the wrong way around: instead of being served in a soup, they are separate – hot or cold. You also get a bowl of stock and dipping sauce, into which you can dip the noodles. It hit the spot yet again!

KUSHIKATSU 串カツ
DEEP-FRIED SKEWERED MEAT AND VEGETABLES

Osaka is also famous for its kushikatsu. You can even sample deep-fried vanilla ice cream at a kushikatsu restaurant. You can deep-fry anything that takes your fancy!

400 g (16 ounces) pork tenderloin, in 4-cm (1 ½-inch) cubes

8 green asparagus spears, in 4-cm (1 ½-inch) pieces

8 shiitake, stems removed, halved

200 g (8 ounces) Camembert, cut into 8 pieces

skewers, 20 to 30 cm (8–12 inches) long

BATTER

2 eggs

200 g (2 cups) flour

200 ml (1 cup) milk

panko

SAUCE

tonkatsu sauce (see p. 203)

Put the eggs, flour and milk in a bowl and whisk to a batter. Place the ingredients on skewers, each time putting two or three pieces of pork on one skewer, three or four pieces of asparagus on another skewer, one or two shiitake on a third skewer and one piece of Camembert on a fourth skewer.

Place batter and panko in separate dishes. Dip each skewer into the batter so that all the ingredients are completely coated. Shake off the surplus batter and then coat the skewers with panko.

Heat the frying oil to 180 °C (350 °F) and fry the skewers until they are golden brown. It is easier to fry them without the frying basket. Do not fry the cheese for too long or it will explode in the pan. Drain the skewers on paper towel and serve immediately with tonkatsu sauce.

IZAKAYA   STANDING BAR

YAEKATSU
EBISU HIGASHI 3-4-13, NANIWA-KU
OSAKA 556-0002
OPEN: 10.30 AM – 9.30 PM
(CLOSED THURSDAYS
AND THIRD WEDNESDAY)

YAKITORI (NEGIMA) 焼き鳥(ねぎま)
FRIED SKEWERED CHICKEN

This is a very popular dish that is also known around the world. Many restaurants in Japan specialise in yakitori. You can try many different cuts of chicken in a variety of ways. Here, we describe a typical dish with leeks.

600 g (24 ounces) chicken leg fillets (skinless, boneless)

2 tablespoons soy sauce

2 tablespoons mirin

1 tablespoon sake

1 tablespoon sugar

2 young leeks, in 3-cm (1-inch) pieces

vegetable oil

shichimi (Japanese seven-spice chile pepper)

Cut the chicken into 3-cm (1-inch) cubes. Mix the soy sauce, mirin, sake and sugar in a bowl until the sugar has completely dissolved. Place the pieces of chicken and leek on the skewers, alternating until you have three pieces of chicken and two pieces of leek per skewer. Heat the oil in a frying pan and fry the skewers for approximately 2 minutes and turn them over. Put a lid on the pan and fry for a further 5 minutes over medium heat. Remove the skewers and add the sauce to the pan. Allow to thicken over medium heat. Return the skewers to the sauce and simmer uncovered. Turn occasionally and allow them to caramelise. Serve with some shichimi.

You can store the sauce for a long time in the refrigerator and also use it in other ways, such as for a wok dish or fried salmon.

Instead of shichimi, you can also use ichimi, which is pure chile powder without the other spices that are in shichimi.

IZAKAYA

STANDING BAR

KAWAYA
SHIROGANE 1-15-7, CHUO-KU
FUKUOKA 810-0012
OPEN DAILY: 5 PM – MIDNIGHT

ODEN おでん
DAIKON, EGG AND FISHCAKE IN STOCK

Japanese winter comfort food! Once winter approaches and the weather turns colder, this dish is served in yatai and izakaya. You will even find it in convenience stores. It really reminds me of a hotpot, especially because it is served with mustard (karashi).

1 medium daikon

1 litre (1 quart) dashi (see p. 196)

3 tablespoons mirin

2 tablespoons light soy sauce

1 tablespoon salt

10 pieces (5 x 2 cm) (2 x 1 inch) deep-fried tofu (atsuage)

4 hard-boiled eggs, peeled

8 Japanese fishcakes

mustard

Peel the daikon and cut it into 3 cm (1 ¼ inch) high cylinders. Slowly bring the dashi to the boil and add the mirin, soy sauce and salt. Add the daikon and cook for 45 minutes. Add the deep-fried tofu, eggs and fishcakes. Serve with mustard.

Oden tastes better if left overnight in the refrigerator and then reheated the next day.

Other optional ingredients for the oden include pumpkin, taro, konnyaku, rice cakes, other types of fishcake, etc..

STANDING BAR   24/7

RAMEN NOODLE BAR

I first came across ramen in the Japanese cult film *Tampopo*. The film inspired me to set up my own noodle bar in Ghent, called *Noedelbar Ramen* (Ramen Noodle Bar). Ramen has now conquered the world. A snippet from history shows us that ramen became hugely popular in Japan after the Second World War. Japan was devastated, the Americans were selling them wheat and the Japanese used it to start making ramen noodles. So what makes ramen so special? It has a certain amount of elasticity, it contains no egg, only water, wheat flour and kansui powder. This is a combination of two types of salt – sodium bicarbonate and potassium carbonate. The name "kansui powder" refers to a Chinese lake, where the water contains these two types of salt. Ramen noodles therefore originate in China.

The noodles are most often served in a stock. In fact, that stock should be pork stock, which is nice and fatty. During a visit to the Ivan Ramen noodle restaurant in Tokyo a few years ago, I came across an alternative: a stock made half with dashi and half with chicken stock. So, for our own ramen restaurant, every week we buy chicken carcasses for making chicken stock, which we mix with dashi. We chose this mixture because people here are not ready for *tonkotsu*, genuine Japanese pork stock.

Furthermore, the reason why the Japanese prefer pork stock is because its very fatty nature means that the stock and therefore the flavour really stick to the noodles.

The word "ramen" is simple, but every chef and ramen stand has its own kodawari (favourite or obsession) and the varieties are endless. If you watch the film *The Ramen Girl*, directed by Robert Allan Ackerman (the film was made in 2008 but it also gives the nod to the famous film *Tampopo*, by Juzo Itami, made in 1985), you could say that the ramen chef is crazy, but the *kodawari* of one dish really can be that serious. Both films portray the huge challenge and passion involved in creating the best ramen. The chef is trying to make his own *hiden* (secret recipe). He spends hours cooking with fresh ingredients in order to produce a delicious and original stock. Virtually every region of Japan has its own version of ramen. Sapporo is known for its miso ramen, in Hiroshima you'll often find *tsukemen* ramen, which are ramen without an actual stock but with a dipping sauce served separately. Fukuoka is known for *tonkotsu* ramen, which means it is in pork stock. It goes without saying that trendy Tokyo has a wealth of creative varieties of ramen.

So how do you define a ramen dish? It is based on the way the ramen is served – in a stock or with the stock served separately – as well as of course in terms of its seasoning or *tare*. *Shio* ramen are flavoured with a salty tare, *shoyu* ramen with a soy tare, and then there's also miso ramen, flavoured with miso paste. A couple of teaspoons of this tare are added to the bowl, stock is poured over, then the noodles, a garnish and a dressing – and there's your dish.

Perhaps what still appeals to me the most is the creativity. Everything in Japanese society is structured and everything in Japanese cuisine is structured. One major exception is ramen. The Japanese attitude to ramen is much more flexible, and so are we at our Ramen noodle bar. At Ramen, our signature dish since day one has been a **vegetarian ramen** (veggie ramen). Every week, we make 50 litres (50 quarts) of vegetable stock using celeriac, leeks, fennel and onion. To provide additional seasoning and to add just a smidgen of fattiness, in our noodle bar we use a mixture of butter, seaweed and shiitake. We mix this with soy tare. The other ingredients are kale, preserved shiitake, spring onions, bamboo shoots and a semi-soft boiled egg.

VEGE RAMEN
ベジラーメン
VEGETARIAN RAMEN

TO MAKE 4 PORTIONS

6 dried shiitake, soaked in water, julienned

4 tablespoons soy sauce

4 tablespoons rice vinegar

4 tablespoons sugar

8 tablespoons shiodare (see p. 204)

4 portions ramen noodles

200 g (8 ounces) kale, finely chopped

2 soy sauce eggs, halved (see p. 202)

4 tablespoons menma (see marinated bamboo shoots on p. 202)

2 spring onions, julienned

1 nori leaf, cut into pieces 6 x 6 cm (2 x 2 inches)

1 quart vegetarian ramen stock (see p. 200)

4 tablespoons shiitake-seaweed butter (see p. 203)

First pickle the shiitake. Put the soy sauce, vinegar and sugar in a saucepan and heat until the sugar has dissolved. Remove from the heat and add the finely chopped shiitake.

Put a tablespoon shiitake-seaweed butter in a noodle bowl. Add two tablespoons shiodare. Do this for all four bowls. Bring the noodles to the boil. Heat up the stock.

Place a portion of noodles in each bowl. Garnish the sides with the kale, shiitake, half an egg and the menma. Pour the stock over the noodles. Garnish with spring onion in the centre of the bowl and a nori leaf to one side.

TONKOTSU RAMEN とんこつラーメン
RAMEN WITH PORK STOCK

The original ramen soup, the star of the entire range: fatty in taste and appearance, a calorie minefield!

500 ml (1 pint) tonkotsu stock

2 portions ramen noodles

2 tablespoons shiodare (see p. 204)

1 tablespoon pork fat

½ teaspoon katsuobushi salt (see p. 199)

200 g (8 ounces) chashu, sliced (see p. 203)

2 spring onions, julienned

a few nori leaves, 8 x 4 cm (3 x 1 ½ inches)

Heat the tonkotsu stock. Boil the noodles in water for a few minutes until cooked.

Put the shiodare into a noodle bowl, add the fat and the katsuobushi salt. Pour a small amount of tonkotsu stock over them so that the fat "melts" a little. Add the noodles and place the finely chopped shiodare over them. Pour the stock over everything. Finish with the strips of spring onion and stand a nori leaf beside the stock. Repeat this for the other portions. Serve as hot as possible.

GANSO NAGAHAMAYA
NAGAHAMA 2-5-38, CHUO-KU
FUKUOKA 810-0072
OPEN DAILY: 4 AM - 1.45 AM

OMURAISU オムライス
OMELETTE ON FRIED RICE

The name is typically "Japlish" – a combination of "omelette" and "rice". Various theories exist as to its origin but, in any event, the dish was "discovered" in the early twentieth century. It is very popular with children (as a topping, they draw characters on the omelettes with ketchup) as well as with adults. Some restaurants specialise in this dish (with numerous variations).

1 small onion, finely minced

1 garlic clove, finely minced

120 g (4 ounces) salted bacon, in small pieces

4 small bowls cooked rice (see p. 198)

5 tablespoons ketchup

1 tablespoon vegetable oil

salt and pepper

OMELETTE

8 eggs

100 ml (½ cup) milk

4 tablespoons Japanese mayonnaise

40 g butter

Heat the oil in a frying pan and fry the onion and garlic for a few minutes. Add the bacon and fry until the bacon is crispy and golden brown. Add the cooked rice and fry everything for 3 to 4 minutes. Then add the ketchup and stir well. Fry for a further 1 minute and season with salt and pepper.

Beat the eggs, milk and mayonnaise in a bowl. Heat the butter in a separate frying pan until half of the butter has melted. Add the egg mixture and fry for 10 seconds. Then stir briefly with a wooden spoon to add some air. Let the bottom set but make sure that the top of the omelette remains runny. Take the pan off the heat.

Spoon the previously fried rice on to four plates and distribute the omelette over the rice. Finish with ketchup and serve hot.

Other sauces can be used instead of ketchup, e.g. Béchamel sauce (as in the photograph).

There is a restaurant in Tokyo called Taimeiken, where you can eat omuraisu that was specially created for the film *Tampopo* by its director, Juzo Itami himself.

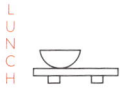

GOKOKU
AKASAKA 1F 2-1-8, CHUO-KU
FUKUOKA 810-0042
OPEN: TUES-SUN, 11 AM – 9.30 PM

KAISEN-DON 海鮮丼
SASHIMI ON RICE BOWL

Typical dish of the places in Japan that have a fish market. If the fish is fresh, it is a special treat! Very simple, colourful and super-tasty!

4 small bowls cooked rice (see p. 198)

500 g (1 pound) mixed fish (salmon, tuna, scallops, salmon roe, etc.)

soy sauce

wasabi

Distribute warm, cooked rice into four small bowls. Cut the pieces of fish into slices approximately 5 mm (¼ inch) thick. Half-fill a bowl with rice. Distribute the fish over the rice and serve with wasabi and soy sauce.

To make the rice bowl more colourful, in addition to fish you can also add other ingredients such as cucumber or dashimaki tamago (see p. 162) etc..

IWASHI NO NITSUKE
イワシの煮付け
SARDINES WITH GINGER

Sardines have always been popular in Japan and are eaten often – as sashimi, as tempura, grilled, etc.. Ginger removes the less pleasant aroma of the fish and adds a tasty aroma. Japan has been enjoying this classic dish for generations.

8 whole sardines, descaled and skinned

MARINADE

4 tablespoons soy sauce

4 tablespoons mirin

4 tablespoons sake

4 tablespoons sugar

200 ml (1 cup) water

3 cm (1 inch) ginger, in thin strips

TO GARNISH

a handful of chives, finely chopped

Cut the sardines into rings 3 cm (1 inch) long. Mix all the marinade ingredients in a pressure cooker. Place the sardines in the marinade and seal the lid. Bring to the boil over a high heat until the cooker is pressurised. Then boil for a further 20 minutes over a low heat. Turn off the heat and leave to stand for 20 minutes. Serve hot or cold with some chives.

Sardines are rich in unsaturated fatty acid and the coenzyme Q10. They are therefore good for the circulation and for cholesterol.

HORENSO NO GOMAAE
ほうれん草の胡麻和え
SPINACH WITH SESAME SAUCE

Along with miso soup, this is one of the first dishes you learn to cook in elementary school. You often see it in bento boxes. Not only is it a pretty green colour, but it is also a major ingredient that contributes to balance in the box. The secret to this recipe is in grinding the sesame seeds while they are still hot. This brings out their full flavour.

500 g (1 pound) spinach
3 tablespoons sesame seeds
2 tablespoons soy sauce
1 tablespoon sugar
1 tablespoon mirin
1 tablespoon dashi (see p. 196)

Blanch the spinach for a few seconds in boiling salted water and drain. Cool in ice-cold water and squeeze out the moisture. Toast the sesame seeds in a pan without oil until they give off a delicious aroma. Tip the sesame seeds into the bowl of a food mixer while they are still hot. Grind the seeds briefly but do not turn them into powder. Add the soy sauce, sugar, mirin and dashi and mix well. Mix the spinach with the sesame sauce and serve.

String beans make a perfect substitute for the spinach.

NIKUDANGO
NO ANKAKE
**MEATBALLS IN
SWEET SAUCE**
SEE P. 99

HORENSO
NO GOMAAE
**SPINACH WITH
SESAME SAUCE**

NIKUDANGO NO ANKAKE
肉団子のあんかけ
MEATBALLS IN SWEET SAUCE

This is very popular with children and is often one of the dishes in a bento box.

MEATBALLS

400 g (16 ounces) minced pork (or mixed minced meat)

1 medium onion, finely chopped

1 tablespoon ginger, finely chopped

1 egg, lightly beaten

5 tablespoons panko

salt and pepper

SAUCE

1 tablespoon mirin

300 ml (1 ½ cups) dashi (see p. 196) or chicken stock (see p. 200)

2 tablespoons soy sauce

2 tablespoons sugar

2 tablespoons potato starch

TO GARNISH

toasted sesame seeds

Mix minced meat, onion, ginger, egg and panko in a large mixing bowl. Add salt and pepper and mix well with your hands. Roll into balls approximately 3 cm (1 ½ inches) thick. Bring water to boil in a pan. Add the balls to the boiling water and boil until they float to the surface (and are therefore cooked). Drain the meatballs and pat dry with paper towel.

Put all the sauce ingredients into a saucepan and mix well with a whisk. Bring slowly to the boil. Stir regularly until the sauce has thickened. Add the meatballs to the sauce and cook for a further 5 minutes over a low heat. Mix carefully. Sprinkle with the sesame seeds and serve.

Sweet and sour sauce also goes perfectly with the meatballs.

MARKET STREET

BENTO

The very word "bento" is so seductive and it gives me a feeling of bliss. It sounds so full of love (even though I usually buy it in a shop) and it is so satisfying (for my stomach). I believe that bento is one of the cornerstones of Japanese cuisine. I am reminded of the Belgian expression, "born with a brick in your stomach" (which means to yearn to build one's own house). The Japanese version of that would be "to have a bento in your stomach" (which actually sounds a bit more normal, I have to say). Simply put, a bento is a "prepared meal to take away", but the combinations are endless. When I went on infant school trips I always took a bento with me that my mother had prepared and later, in middle school, I took one with me from home almost every day. Bento is ubiquitous and available everywhere in Japan: in stations, convenience stores, supermarkets and special bento shops, where you can buy them hot and freshly-made. Convenience stores in Japan are more than just what the name suggests. They try to distinguish themselves from the competition with their culinary ideas and creations. When I worked in Japan, I sometimes bought a bento at lunch time from a pop-up stall, just as Tom and Luk did when they visited Japan. They are colourful, healthy and tasty. Although I don't know and can't see the chef, his message is clear: "Enjoy your meal and I hope I am making you happy."

When director Hirokazu Koreeda came to the Ghent Film Fest a couple of years ago, I prepared a bento box for him. Later, he said that he had really enjoyed it at night, when he could not sleep because of jet lag. To promote his latest film, he flew from one film festival to another and he had just arrived from New York. He particularly wanted to come to Ghent again, he said, because the festival and the city continue to occupy a special place in his heart since he won the prize for best film with his masterpiece, *Nobody Knows*.

Eating bento has a long history in Japan. As far back as the sixteenth century, it was served in the typical box shape still used today and enjoyed during tea ceremonies or gatherings such as *hanami* (the cherry blossom festival). Since the seventeenth and eighteenth centuries, bento has been eaten during the kabuki or noh theatre intermissions and, even then, many recipe books were devoted entirely to the art of bento.

The bento tradition, originally a symbol of motherly love, is therefore highly developed in Japan and yet it continues to develop in the most diverse forms and varieties. This can also be seen in current words such as *eki-ben* or station bento (many stations in Japan have their own specialities), ai-sai-bento, or "lunch box of beloved wife", which is what a husband calls the bento that his loving wife has made for him, kyara-ben, or character bento, where cute figures from animated films, etc., are used as decoration, and many more.

POTETO SALADA ポテトサラダ
POTATO SALAD

A very popular snack in Japan and a common item in bento boxes. In Japan, Tom ate this salad in a roll.

3 medium potatoes, unpeeled

1 medium carrot

1 egg

half a cucumber, seeds removed

1 onion, sliced into rings

6 tablespoons Japanese mayonnaise

salt and pepper to taste

Boil the potatoes in their skins until cooked. Do the same with the carrots and the egg (hard-boiled). Slice the cucumber and the onion and sprinkle with salt. Leave them for 10 minutes and then rinse in plenty of cold water. This will draw the moisture out of the onion and the cucumber and make them crunchy.

Peel the potatoes and the egg. Blend the potatoes in a mixer but do not blend them entirely; save some pieces. Chop the carrots and mix with the potatoes. Mash the hard-boiled egg and add it to the mixture. Allow this mixture to cool. Once cooled, add the finely sliced cucumber and onion. Mix in the mayonnaise. Season with salt and pepper

MENTAIKO TO SHISO NO TEMPURA 明太子と紫蘇の天ぷら
COD ROE TEMPURA WITH PERILLA LEAVES

Frying fish roe is certainly not an everyday technique in Japan but, for this dish, we are happy to make an exception. The combination of the spicy mentaiko and the typically Japanese perilla leaves (shiso) produces a powerful, unique taste. You'll also enjoy the contrast in textures between the crispy outside and the soft, raw inside.

A good sake goes best with this dish...

4 pieces (approximately 120 g (4 ounces)) mentaiko (spicy cod roe)

4 large perilla leaves (shiso)

BATTER

60 g (½ cup) flour
50 g (⅓ cup) potato starch
100 ml (½ cup) water
1 teaspoon Japanese mayonnaise

Prick the skin around the mentaiko so that it does not burst during frying. Roll each piece of mentaiko in perilla leaves and secure the leaves with wooden cocktail sticks. Combine all the ingredients for the batter in a bowl and dip the mentaiko rolls in the batter so that they are fully coated. Heat the frying oil to 180 °C (350 °F) and fry the rolls for 2 minutes. The outside turns crispy but the inside must remain raw. Serve immediately.

Perilla leaf tempura on its own is also delicious.

SAKE AND SHOCHU

You can tell that I'm a "child of the Showa period" when I write about *Sake to namida to otoko to onna* (Sake, tears, men and women), the most famous song by Eigo Kawashima, originally from Osaka. Not just this song, but also the image of sake in general makes me think somewhat sentimentally about how Japan used to be. The Showa period refers to the reign of Emperor Hirohito, which ended in 1989. The end of this era happened to coincide with the start of big economic and social changes in Japan, and for me personally with the end of my childhood, which is why I feel such nostalgia. I associate the song with the image of sake that remains with me from my childhood: a drink that exhausted men used to drink after work. The sake had to be heated up and was drunk in sips from a small bowl. Japanese sake is one of the few alcoholic drinks that can be more tasty when heated up. It is said that *hitohada* (body temperature) is ideal for warm sake. But, depending on the season, it is sometimes heated to 50 to 55 °C (120 to 130 °F).

Aside from that sentimental image, sake also represents something pure and "divine" to me. In Japan, you cannot drink alcohol until the age of twenty but the first day of the year was an exception for me. Every year, I had to drink *otoso* (spiced hot sake) from a special *urushi*-laquered bowl in order to chase the evil from the year and to wish for a long and healthy life. Various types of sake are available, depending on the rice polishing ratio, the addition of natural alcohol, whether or not it is pasteurised, etc.. One of the best known types is *junmai-shu*, brewed using only rice, water and *koji* mould (as yeast), without the addition of alcohol. Of course, entire books could be written about brewing fine, pure sake. It is in any event a very long process and is carried out only by men. I am reminded of the wonderful documentary, *The Birth of Saké* (2015), about an artisan brewer in Kanazawa. Since watching it, I always remember the difficult circumstances and the sacrifices people have to make for it and I am still thankful whenever I am able to taste hand-crafted sake. Sake is also an essential aspect of Japanese cuisine. It is often used as *kakushiaji* (which literally means "hidden taste"). Sake is therefore a kind of "miracle drug" that can be combined with all kinds of ingredients. Sake not only purifies a less pleasant fish or meat smell, but it also makes the meat tender and gives umami to the ingredients. You can also steam virtually anything with sake: chicken, pork, clams, scampi, vegetables, etc.. Add a dash of soy sauce and your Japanese meal is ready!

In Japan, the word "sake" often refers simply to "alcoholic drink" in general. Shochu is also a typically Japanese drink that is sometimes confused with sake and also has a long history as "the people's drink". Sake is brewed from rice, while shochu is distilled from various ingredients. You can therefore translate "sake" as "rice wine", while shochu comes in many different types: rice, wheat, sweet potato, brown sugar, soba, chestnut, etc.. Many people think that sake has a high alcohol percentage, but usually it is 13-19%, while shochu is stronger (20-45%). Shochu is also drunk in various different ways: with ice cubes, diluted with cold or hot water, mixed with Japanese tea, or as a sweet cocktail. My favourite is "on the rocks", but diluted with hot water is perhaps easier on the stomach. Of course, everyone has their preferences but it is said that shochu does not give you a bad hangover – and that is certainly true for me.

In Japan, people say *sake ni nomareru*. Literally translated, this means "to be drunk by the sake". So the sake drinks you up! And if you are drunk by the sake, you have lost control. So everything in moderation. There's an old Chinese saying that goes, "Drunk in moderation, alcohol is the best medicine". The same is true for sake and shochu.

BASIL RAMEN バジルラーメン
PESTO RAMEN

Ramen is not bound by hard-and-fast rules. In Tom's noodle bar he serves ramen with Singapore laksa pasta as a base. Below is a version with pesto. The good thing about ramen soups is that you can experiment as much as you want and can add different flavours.

240 ml (1 cup) chicken stock (see p. 200)

240 ml (1 cup) dashi (see p. 196)

2 portions ramen noodles

2 tablespoons basildare (see p. 204)

1 tablespoon chicken fat

1 tablespoon pork fat

½ teaspoon katsuobushi salt (see p. 199)

200 g (8 ounces) chashu, in slices (see p. 203)

2 spring onions, julienned

a few nori leaves, 8 x 4 cm (3 x 1 ½ inches)

Heat the chicken stock and the dashi in a saucepan. Boil the noodles in water for a few minutes until cooked. Place the basildare in a noodle bowl, add the fat and the katsuobushi salt. Pour over a small amount of the chicken dashi so that the fat "melts" a little.

Add the noodles and place the finely chopped chashu on top. Pour the stock over everything. Garnish with the spring onion strips and stand a nori leaf upright beside the stock. Repeat this for the second portion. Serve as hot as possible.

RAMEN UNARI
NAKASU 3-6-23, HAKATA-KU
FUKUOKA 810-0801
OPEN: MON-SAT, 6 PM – 6 AM

TSUKEMEN つけ麺
DIPPING NOODLES

Ramen, but in reverse. The noodles are served separately alongside the stock or dipping sauce. The dipping sauce can be hot or cold; this makes a wonderful summer dish. At the Afuri ramen stand in Tokyo, the dipping sauce is garnished with a shoot of yuzu to give a deliciously fresh taste!

DIPPING SAUCE

1 tablespoon sesame oil

3 cm (1 inch) ginger, finely minced

2 cloves garlic

1 tablespoon tobanjan paste

250 g (8 ounces) belly pork, in strips

100 ml (½ cup) mentsuyu (see p. 28)

250 ml water

NOODLES

1 package ramen noodles

1 soft-boiled egg

50 g (2 ounces) chashu chopped pork (see p. 203)

20 g (1 ounce) bamboo shoots (menma) (see p. 202)

First, make the dipping sauce. Heat the sesame oil in a pan and then add the ginger and garlic. After a few seconds, add the tobanjan paste. After 10 seconds, add the pork and stir until browned. Add the mentsuyu and the water and bring to the boil. Strain the dipping sauce. Leave to cool if you want to serve the dipping sauce cold. Keep hot if you want to serve the dipping sauce hot.

Cook the noodles according to the packet directions. Rinse in cold water. Arrange the noodles, egg, pork and the menma on a plate. Serve with the cold or hot dipping sauce.

ON THE ROAD

From Fukuoka, we took the *shinkansen* (high-speed train) to Kunamoto. Every train station in Japan is a true food heaven, with bento boxes, takeaway sushi, food halls, etc.. So at Kunamoto station, we again stocked up with plenty of food and we took it with us as we boarded the bus to Aso, where we wanted to visit the local volcano. Since it turned out that this volcano was about ten kilometres from our hotel, we decided to have a hitch-hiking competition. We divided into two groups to see who would be the first to hitch-hike to the volcano. Ciska, Laurens and I (we assumed that a group of three that included a woman would be picked up more quickly than three men) against Pieterjan and Benoit. And we were right; after just a few minutes we got a lift. But when our driver passed the other two soon after that, he stopped for them too. In other words, our competition was a failure! Eventually, we all drove up together.

Yet another unbelievable example of Japanese hospitality: our driver wasn't intending to go anywhere near the volcano, but took us there and even waited an hour for us so he could take us back to the village of Aso, out of hospitality and pride. Once we were back in Aso, we even found ourselves invited to his house. His wife had made fried and **steamed dumplings** (*gyoza*) for us, with a very strong garlic flavour. So there we sat, eating gyoza with a Japanese couple, in their living room, with beers and sake, and a photo of a sumo wrestler (their son!) on the wall. And before we could start to feel uncomfortable in such surroundings, our host took us back to our hotel. That hotel was the Aso Base Backpackers Hotel and I recommend it: twenty euros per night for a state-of-the-art dormitory with curtains, books, etc.. Yet further proof that Japan can also be affordable. In the evening, our host's wife came to bring us a photograph of us all in their living room. It was a really great experience.

On the journey back to Fukuoka, the five of us went for the genuine *onsen* experience. We took the bus to Kurokawa, one of the most beautiful onsen villages in Japan. Between eleven and four, we went from one spa to another in Kurokawa. Some were outside, others covered, some were in caves and some were even for both men and women... where we sat stark naked with our colleagues! It's a little different from being in a steamy kitchen!

All the train stations have one or more bakeries – which are actually everywhere in Japan. They may just be the best bakeries in the world. In Kurokawa, we tested our taste buds extensively with crispy apple cake and **Japanese sponge cake** (*kasutera*). It had been a long time since I'd had such delicious cake! The combinations are sometimes a little strange, but always delicious. What would you say to a **curry bread with beef** (*curry pan*) or a bun with soba or udon noodles?

Our next travel destination was Hiroshima. It was already late when we arrived and found the doors of the famous Ueno Anagomeshi restaurant closed. They have been grilling conger eel there for one hundred and fifteen years. But it was completely shut up and there was nothing we could do about it! The next morning, we crossed the water to Miyajima and it was, in a word, fantastic. A magical place with the most photographed image in Japan: the red gate in the water. Taking the cable car, we climbed part of the six-hundred-metre high mountain. We continued along a pilgrims' route, right to the summit. From there, we enjoyed a beautiful view of the Japanese Inland Sea and we could see right over Hiroshima. It looked phenomenal, especially in its autumnal colours. What made our experience even more enjoyable was that we had decided to make the journey in the morning, when there are few people there. Strolling along the pilgrims' route was also a special and very spiritual experience. Once we got back down, we found another mountain – of street food: Benoit ate a **steamed bun** (*nikuman*), while the rest of us feasted on oysters and **fish-shaped**

cakes with sweetened adzuki beans (taiyaki). I saved my appetite so that finally I could try the grilled eel at the one-hundred-and-fifteen-year-old restaurant. This time, it was open but there was a two-hour wait for a seat. So we went for takeaway and, jumping on the train with my grilled eel, headed for Hiroshima central station. That **grilled eel / conger eel** (unagi / anago no kabayaki), served on a bed of rice with some pickles, was pure umami.

The ultimate Hiroshima dish is **savoury pancakes with cabbage** (okonomiyaki) or the Japanese equivalent of pizza. It's a poor man's meal dating from after the Second World War, based on cabbage, flour, water and egg. This mixture is used to cook thin pancakes on a griddle. By the way, do you know why our food trip took us to Hiroshima? So that we could order okonomiyaki on every floor of Okonomi-mura – a building with fifteen okonomiyaki stalls spread over three floors. Okonomiyaki are true works of art. The five of us sat at a counter in each one, gazing at the dancing bonito flakes on the hot, bacon-sprinkled pancake. You use a spatula to divide this okonomiyaki into portions and, after three portions, you could literally have rolled us out the door!

About half an hour by train from Hiroshima is a sake village, where you can taste samples everywhere. Its name is Saijo and it needs no further explanation. We really did sample *everywhere*, among the chimneys of the traditional distilleries – Fukubijin and Kamoizumi – and getting drunk on sake makes you so mellow.... The next day we took the boat to Imabari, on the other side of the Seto islands. All these little islands are linked by huge bridges, so you can also drive to them. But that ferry and its little engine manoeuvring back and forth among the islands – that was a real shock to the system after all the strict train timetables of the previous days. One of the islands also turned out to be covered in scented yuzu and lemon trees. Magical! We then took the bus: crossing from one island to another over all those long bridges, it was as if were driving over the Golden Gate Bridge ten times, but in a tropical environment. It was spectacular!

Another day, another destination: Marugame, known for its udon noodles. Something hilarious happened to us there. As I already mentioned, it is really a good idea to book your hotels in advance in Japan. Even if you go into a hotel with plenty of empty rooms, they still look at you strangely if you say that you want a room. Still, I had taken a chance with not booking anything in Marugame and I again discovered that "that's not the thing to do". Everything was full. Someone on the street suggested, in all seriousness, that we pitch a tent beside the railway line. We thanked him sincerely and then, when we did eventually find a guest house, the lady owner pushed two microphones into our hands and we realised we had ended up in... a karaoke room. A two-person karaoke room no less. First, we laughed our heads of for about half an hour, then we went out for a drink, and I'm still not clear how all five of us finally managed to fall asleep in there.

Public life in Japan is so stressful that people have a strong tendency to create their own imaginary worlds. This tendency can be seen in "love hotels", for example, where people rent a room for intimacy, as well as for gaming or disco dancing. It's all about renting a couple of hours of private space, away from the impersonal pressure. Evidently, karaoke rooms are part of this concept, where you can sing karaoke to your heart's content.
And what do you do when you wake up in a karaoke room? You jump on the train to the art island of Naoshima. Tadao Ando, an architect of whom I am a big fan, has built several museums there. Nursing our hangovers, we visited the Benesse House and the Chichu Art Museum. Coincidentally, a triennial was underway. That day was entirely devoted to art and, while my colleagues were waiting for the ferry, I paid a quick visit to a spa. Yep, the karaoke room did not have a shower!

GYOZA 餃子
FRIED AND STEAMED DUMPLINGS

A fabulous snack! With a fried, crispy side and a soft, steamed part on the other side.

⅕ Chinese cabbage

10 g finely grated ginger

½ packet finely chopped Chinese chives

400 g (1 pound) minced pork

200 g (½ pound) scampi, peeled and finely chopped

½ tablespoon sake

½ tablespoon sesame oil

1 tablespoon light soy sauce

¼ teaspoon sugar

½ teaspoon finely ground black pepper

gyoza dough sheets

gyoza dipping sauce (see p. 202)

Cut the Chinese cabbage into pieces, preferably the soft part. Place in a colander and sprinkle with salt. Place a plate on top with a weight and leave to stand for 1 hour. This draws the moisture out of the cabbage. Rinse the cabbage in plenty of water and wring out. Mix the cabbage with the ginger, chives, minced meat and scampi.

Combine the sake, sesame oil, light soy sauce, sugar and pepper in a small bowl. Now add to the minced meat, cabbage and scampi mixture. Mix well.

Hold one gyoza wrapper in your hand. Moisten the top of the sheet with one finger of the other hand. Using a teaspoon, place a small amount of the mixture in the middle of the gyoza wrapper. Fold the wrapper to seal it, then fold the top over a couple of times and crimp it.

Fry the gyoza for 30 seconds in a dash of oil until it is crispy underneath. Now get the lid of the pan ready. Add 100 ml (½ cup) water to the pan and immediately cover with the lid. The gyoza are now being steamed. Remove the pan once all the water has evaporated and the bottom of the dumplings looks crispy. Serve with gyoza sauce.

Endless variations are possible. Create your own filling and style!

当店は**食券制**でございます。

元祖長浜屋台

KASUTERA カステラ
JAPANESE SPONGE CAKE

The name comes from the Portuguese word *castela* (which in turn refers to the Spanish place name Castille) and is inspired by cakes and sweets from Portugal that were introduced in Nagasaki in the sixteenth century. The fact that back then no dairy products were used in its preparation probably explains why kasutera developed into one of the most popular, best known and most typical sweet Japanese dishes. Nagasaki is still known for its kasutera. The unique, silky soft texture of the cake is obtained by wrapping the cake, just after baking, in plastic wrap and then storing it overnight in the refrigerator after cooling.

30 ml (⅛ cup) milk
1 tablespoon honey
2 eggs
75 g (⅓ cup) sugar
75 g (⅔ cup) flour, sifted
1 tablespoon vegetable oil

Preheat the oven to 180 °C (350 °F). Heat the milk and the honey in a pan until the honey has completely dissolved. Separate the eggs and beat the whites with a mixer until stiff. Gradually mix the sugar into the egg whites and make a stiff meringue mix. Put the meringue in a large bowl and add the flour. Mix carefully with a spatula. Add the milk mixture and the oil. Mix well until the batter is smooth. Line a cake tin (approximately 20 cm x 7 cm (8 x 3 inches)) with greaseproof paper. Pour the batter into the tin and tap the base of the tin on the work surface a few times to release any air bubbles.

Bake the cake in the oven for 10 minutes at 180 °C (350 °F) and then for another 20 minutes at 150 °C (300 °F). In the meantime, place a piece of microwave-safe cling film about 30 cm (12 inches) long on the work surface. Take the cake out of the oven and leave to cool slightly. Turn the tin over (when the cake tin is no longer red hot) so that the top of the cake touches the cling film. Remove the cake tin and roll the cake up in the cling film while the cake is still hot. Place the cake on the work surface with the top facing up. Leave the cake to stand for 24 hours at room temperature. Remove the film and cut the cake into slices 2 to 3 cm (1 to 1 ½ inches) thick and serve.

The edges are the best, so keep them for yourself. ;-)

CURRY PAN カレーパン
CURRY BREAD WITH BEEF

From a Japanese bakery! Below is a simplified version.

2 tablespoons peanut oil

2 medium onions, halved and sliced

200 g (8 ounces) beef, finely sliced

300 ml (1 ½ cups) water

half a cube of Japanese curry

2 tablespoons soy sauce

1 teaspoon corn starch

FOR THE BUN

200 g (2 cups) pancake mix

65 g (2 ounces) yoghurt

1 tablespoon Japanese mayonnaise

3 tablespoons flour

1 egg

150 g (1 cup) panko

oil for frying

First make the filling. Put the peanut oil in a wok. Fry the onion until soft. Add the beef and fry until brown. Now add the water. Bring to the boil and dissolve a curry cube in the liquid. Season to taste with soy sauce. Add the corn starch and allow to thicken. Leave to cool. The mixture must have a thick, firm consistency.

Put the pancake mix in a mixing bowl. Add the yoghurt and mix together. Mix the mayonnaise with one tablespoon of water in a separate bowl. Add this mixture to the pancake and yoghurt mixture.

Dust the work surface with flour. Divide the dough into small 5-cm (2-inch) balls. Use a rolling pin to flatten the balls into round discs. Using a tablespoon, scoop 2 spoonfuls of the curried meat mixture into the centre of each round disc. Lift up the edges and seal. Sprinkle more flour over the balls.

Lightly beat the egg in a bowl. Put the panko in a second bowl. Heat the frying oil to 175 °C (350 °F). Immerse the balls in the egg mixture then carefully press them into the panko and fry them for 3 minutes until cooked.

MARKET STREET

NIKUMAN 肉まん
STEAMED BUN

DOUGH

300 g (3 cups) flour

1 teaspoon dried yeast

½ teaspoon salt

1 teaspoon baking powder

2 tablespoons sugar

1 tablespoon peanut oil

170 ml (¾ cup) water

FILLING

⅛ Chinese cabbage, hard parts removed, finely chopped

½ teaspoon salt

300 g (10 ounces) minced pork

2 spring onions, in rings

4 dried shiitake, soaked 15 minutes, hard parts removed, finely chopped

3 cm (1 inch) ginger, peeled and finely grated

1 tablespoon sesame oil

1 tablespoon soy sauce

1 tablespoon sake

1 teaspoon sugar

½ teaspoon black pepper

1 tablespoon corn starch

6 tablespoons water

First make the dough. Place the flour, yeast, salt, baking powder, sugar and oil in a mixing bowl. Gradually add the water and knead to a smooth, firm mass. Shape the dough into a long roll. Cut into 4-5 cm (1 ½-2 inch) pieces. Dust the work surface with a little extra flour. Roll the pieces into balls. Place the balls on a greased baking tray. Cover with a tea towel and leave to rise for one hour.

Now make the filling. Place the cabbage in a colander, sprinkle with salt and place a weight on top. Leave to stand for 30 minutes. Then rinse abundantly with water and wring out the cabbage. Add the minced meat, spring onion, shiitake and ginger. Season to taste with sesame oil, soy sauce, sake, sugar, salt and pepper. Mix the corn starch with the water and add to the pork mixture. Knead everything together.

Dust the work surface with flour. Take a ball of dough and flatten it with your hand. Spoon one-and-a-half tablespoons of filling into the centre of the flattened ball of dough. Lift the edges of the dough and seal them to create a closed ball. Line a steamer basket with greaseproof paper. You may want to make holes in it so that the steam can escape. Bring water to the boil and steam the buns for 10 minutes until cooked.

Delicious for breakfast!

MARKET STREET

24/7

TAIYAKI たい焼き
CAKE WITH SWEETENED ADZUKI BEANS

Since the Meiji period (end of the nineteenth century), a cake mould in the shape of a gilt-head bream (dorade) has been used in Japan for this cake. Gilt-head bream in Japanese is "tai", which also means luck in the sense of "mede-tai". As a result, this cake is also a symbol that is supposed to bring good luck. The cake also reminds Miho of her student days, when she lived next door to a shop that sold cakes like this… It has such a delicious smell that, to this day, Miho cannot resist freshly-baked taiyaki.

BATTER

100 g (1 cup) flour

1 teaspoon bicarbonate of soda

80 ml (⅓ cup) water

50 ml (⅕ cup) milk

½ tablespoon sugar

salt

FILLING

200 g (7 oz) sweetened adzuki beans (see p. 206)

Mix all the batter ingredients together in a bowl. Cover and leave to rest for 1 hour in the refrigerator.

Heat the taiyaki iron (type of waffle iron in the shape of a fish) and rub with oil. Pour the batter on to the hot iron and place the adzuki beans in the middle of the fish shape. Spoon the batter over the beans and close the taiyaki iron. Bake 3 to 5 minutes until the pastries are golden brown. Serve immediately.

You can also use thick pastry custard instead of the sweetened adzuki beans.

MARKET STREET

NARUTO TAIYAKI HONPO
ASAKUSABASHI 1-9-1, TAITO-KU
TOKIO 111-0053
OPEN: 10 AM - 10 PM

UNAGI / ANAGO NO KABAYAKI うなぎ/あなごの蒲焼

JAPANESE-STYLE GRILLED EEL / CONGER EEL

It has long been said that eating unagi during the hot, humid Japanese summer will give you great stamina. When you sweat, you can easily become deficient in vitamin B and a lack of vitamin B leads to fatigue. Unagi contains a lot of protein and vitamin B. Unagi no kabayaki is often served over white rice as well as in a bento box.

3 eel fillets (bone removed without cutting through the back)

400 ml (2 cups) soy sauce

200 ml (1 cup) mirin

2 tablespoons sake

2 tablespoons sugar

Szechuan pepper

Preheat the oven on grill setting. Cut the eel into 10-cm (4-inch) pieces. Grill the eel in the oven until crispy and golden brown. Turn and grill until 80% cooked. Remove the eel from the oven.

Mix the soy sauce, mirin, sake and sugar in a pan and place on a high heat. Turn down the heat to low when the mixture starts to boil and add the eel. Cook gently for approximately 5 minutes.

Remove the eel from the sauce and grill again on both sides very briefly in the preheated oven, so that a crust forms. Remove the eel from the oven and place it on a serving platter. Spoon a small amount of sauce over the eel and garnish with some Szechuan pepper.

Eel is rich not only in vitamin B, but also in vitamins A and E and in omega-3 fatty acids. In other words, it is good for your brain, your cholesterol and for the appearance of your skin and eyes. Eating eel also strengthens the immune system. Salt-water eel (anago) is prepared in the same way. Salt-water eel contains less fat and has a lighter taste. Hiroshima is famous for its salt-water eel.

UENO ANAGOMESHI
MIYAJIMAGUCHI 1-5-11, HATSUKAICHI
HIROSHIMA 739-0411
OPEN: 10 AM – 7 PM

OKONOMIYAKI: HIROSHIMA-YAKI AND OSAKA-YAKI

I was born and brought up in Osaka but at home we always ate *Hiroshima-yaki*, in other words, okonomiyaki Hiroshima-style. That's because my parents came from Hiroshima. So, our favourite okonomiyaki restaurant in Osaka also followed the Hiroshima style. It was located in Bishoen, close to the busy district of Tennoji, about twenty minutes' drive from our house. We always went there without booking and often had to wait for a table. Manga books were always lying around for the people who were waiting. The restaurant was very small, no more than a counter in fact, and it was right underneath the Japan Railway tracks. For that reason, the rattle of trains passing overhead is a nostalgic memory for me.

This okonomiyaki restaurant was described in various magazines as one of the best in the city (which was far from self-evident for Hiroshima-yaki in Osaka), but the atmosphere of "small and friendly" never changed. In front of our eyes, on the other side of the counter, two cheerful sisters cooked their food while chattering non-stop. They called my father *nii-chan* (brother) and my mother *nee-chan* (sister). My father was a regular there even before he married. Once the okonomiyaki we had ordered was ready, the sisters always asked my parents if their three daughters wanted mustard (which is in fact not so customary with okonomiyaki; I only learned to eat mustard and wasabi much later). Every time, they were surprised at how big the girls (i.e. my sisters and I) had grown. The daughter of one of the two sisters married an American and moved to the United States. To me back then, as a child, that sounded so far away from Japan and I could barely imagine how she would survive there, with a different language. She looked so free and radiant, with her long hair, and I can still remember that I idolised her a little. Now, here I am myself in Ghent, writing about them in a foreign language, with music in the background by Ryuichi Sakamoto, of whom I have been a fan since I was a child and whom I met this year in Ghent. You just never know the things that might happen in your life.

A few years ago, I went back to that restaurant. The son of one of the sisters had taken over the business but, in fact, nothing had changed. She was still there, grilling, and she cried out in wonder at how grown-up I had become. When we bade farewell, she gave me a big bag of dashi (see p. 196) because that was what her daughter always took back to the US after a visit to Japan.

My first experience with *Osaka-yaki* came via the *yatai* (food stalls) at summer festivals, i.e. as genuine street food. The ingredients and sauce used for both types of frying are approximately the same and both taste delicious but, to my mind, they are different dishes. The main difference is that, when making Hiroshima-yaki, the ingredients are not mixed with the batter, whereas they are when making Osaka-yaki. For Hiroshima-yaki, a thin layer of batter is poured onto a *teppan* (iron griddle), just like a very thin pancake (a French *crêpe* is perhaps more like it) and then the *gu* (contents) is placed on top. This means fine, length-wise cut strands of white cabbage, other vegetables and meat or fish; the possibilities are endless.. For the Osaka-yaki, all the ingredients are first mixed into the batter and then the entire mixture is fried. You can see the difference between the two when you cut into the fried okonomiyaki: in one, the ingredients are in layers and in the other everything is mixed together.

At our favourite restaurant, I could also choose whether I wanted noodles on top as well, which is often done with Hiroshima-yaki, but is not necessary. *Okonomi* means "what you prefer, your own taste" so, as the name suggests, the choice is up to you. I think Hiroshima-yaki is a little lighter because it uses less batter. Although it can become pretty heavy when you put noodles on top! In any event, okonomiyaki is a tasty and comforting meal for anyone wanting to satisfy their hunger quickly.

OKONOMIYAKI (HIROSHIMA-YAKI)

お好み焼き（広島焼き）

SAVOURY JAPANESE PANCAKES WITH CABBAGE (HIROSHIMA-STYLE)

bonito flakes

600-700 g (20-24 ounces) white cabbage, finely chopped

250 g (9 ounces) beansprouts

50 g (2 ounces) spring onion, in rings

200 g (8 ounces) unsalted bacon slices

4 eggs

300-500 g (10-17 ounces) yellow noodles (cooked)

BATTER

200 ml (2 cups) flour

200 ml (1 cup) water

TO GARNISH

tonkatsu sauce (see p. 203)

Japanese mayonnaise

aonori (very fine flakes of dried seaweed)

In a bowl, mix flour and water for the batter. Heat the teppan or a frying pan with a little oil and pour the batter on to the hot surface. Make it into a round shape, 12 to 15 cm (5 to 6 inches). Sprinkle a few bonito flakes on the batter. Put one quarter of the cabbage, beansprouts, spring onion and bacon on top. Pour 2 to 3 tablespoons of batter on top of this in a circular movement. Flip the pancake (use two spatulas if necessary) and continue frying until the vegetables are tender. Do not press down excessively.

Heat another frying pan, break an egg into it and break up the yolk but keep its round shape. Fry the egg quickly and place the noodles on top of it before the egg has set (the noodles may also be fried in advance). Then place the previously fried pancake on top. Flip the whole thing so that the egg side is on top. Serve hot with garnish.

You can also use Chinese cabbage instead of white cabbage. The frying time will then be shorter because the leaves are thinner. Many other ingredients are possible, as is explained in the recipe for Osaka-style okonomiyaki (see p. 177). In Japan, even cheese, kimchi, slivers of potato and other ingredients are used.

OKONOMI-MURA
SHINTENCHI 5-13, NAKA-KU
HIROSHIMA 730-0034
OPEN DAILY: 11.30 AM – MIDNIGHT

EAT 'TILL YOU DROP

On our first evening in Osaka, we found ourselves in the Tengachaya neighbourhood. Laurens had a girlfriend there, Yuka, with whom we could stay. We had a small apartment to ourselves, with three small rooms. Tengachaya is an old, popular neighbourhood, which the Japanese regard as "dangerous", but that can be taken with a large pinch of salt. It's just somewhat less clean. We immediately immersed ourselves in the Tenma neighbourhood, with its wide range of *tachinomiyas*, or "standing bars" – eateries where you eat standing up. For me, this was the most radical experience of the entire trip. One of the dishes most unique to Osaka is *horumon* – tripe. There's even an expression that goes, "Everything they throw away in Tokyo, they eat in Osaka". Anyway, we found ourselves in a bar with a name that sounded like Tsukie – a *tachinomiya* where *horumon* was served. We ate some unbelievable things there! The fourth stomach of a cow, the uterus of a cow, the Achilles tendon of a cow... All washed down with generous amounts of alcohol, of course. The offal is served on plates and you grill it yourself over wood fires arranged on the bar... I can't say I'm crazy about tripe, but you do it for fun as much as anything. Let's just give it a try! It's hard to describe the atmosphere in these standing bars, with all the *salarymen*, the office workers, suddenly letting their hair down a bit – and making a lot of noise.

On the second day, Tomoko and Miho arrived. Tomoko took us straight to the business district for lunch. Lunch is a fascination for me anyway, because it has to be quick. I was incredibly surprised to see how, on the stroke of twelve, all these people came outside to eat. It reminded me of midtown New York, around Park Avenue, where all the offices empty around midday and people head for the food trucks. Short on time, but rich in choice. I felt that same vibe in Osaka, although here they had small stalls with people selling **lunch boxes** (*bento boxes*), rather than food trucks. Packaging and presentation take pride of place – even a bento box is made into an array of beautiful colours – but taste is equally important. Rice, noodles, sushi and side dishes – the possibilities are endless. The box always involves an attractive interplay of tastes and colours in a compartmentalised box. We went into a lunch place and shared a couple of plates of **thinly sliced beef with egg** (*gyuuniku no tamago-toji*) and **steak with Japanese savoury sauce** (*gyu steeki wafu-sosu*).

We willingly followed Tomoko to a shopping street, the Tenjinbashi Market, an arcade stretching for 3 kilometres. This must be the longest street market in the world, I thought. Tomoko led us to a Japanese tea house on this shopping street. It was very modern and zen-like in terms of its interior. There, it was sweet treats all round: **Japanese green tea latte** (*matcha latte*), **shaved ice with green tea syrup** (*matcha kakigori*), **cold green tea** (*tsumetai ryokucha*) and **cakes filled with mascarpone and red bean paste** (*mascarpone no monaka*). Tea, and green tea in particular, is an essential part of Japanese culture.

After our half-hour of chilling, we continued our journey: we discovered unbelievably good things on every side of that three kilometre-long market: fish shops, delis, the list is endless, just like the street. We made our first stop for **smoked eggs** (*kunsei tamago*) and then again for a **croquette with minced meat** (*niku korokke*) at a croquette bar. A little bit further along, we found ourselves in a tofu place, run by a particularly friendly man. He was very passionate about what he did, which is often the case in Japan. He was a genuinely delightful man! He had just made **soy milk pudding** (*tonyu purin*), with vanilla and chocolate, and he said we just *had* to try it. He had also made sardines with ginger and **Japanese omelette** (*dashimaki tamago*). These are lightly sweetened and, once cooked, they are rolled up in layers. The 70-year-old man was extremely proud of his merchandise – you could see it in his face. He radiated a sense of honour in his profession.

We wanted to thank our hostess, Yuka, again for opening her home to us, so we bought six dishes from a deli: **meatballs in sweet sauce** (niku dango), **European/Dutch-style aubergines** (nasu no orandani), **rice with hijiki seaweed** (hijiki gohan) and **okra and chicken salad** (okura to toriniku no salada). We took these dishes as takeaways in little containers, back to "our" neighbourhood of Tengachaya so that we could have a cosy evening eating them, together with Yuka and her husband. It was a family-style evening with beer, sake and shochu, an alcoholic drink made from potatoes. We ended the evening with a cake that Yuka herself had made for Laurens' birthday. He was also given a knife from Sakai, a village near Osaka where knife-makers have lived for many centuries. Of course, Yuka's gift was beautifully wrapped, because the Japanese definitely understand the art of wrapping. I have bought things in Japan that were so beautifully wrapped that I did not dare open them.

The next day, we travelled through Namba, the heart of Osaka. Tomoko took us to the Kuromon Market, a very busy district with enough street food to last a lifetime. You can choose fish from a tank and have it grilled in front of you, you can have ramen, oysters, meat, baked goods, etc.. A friendly stall-holder let us try **miso-marinated and baked salmon** (kake no saikyo yaki). Great! We wandered towards Amerikamura, which is a comical name for the hipster district of Osaka. There, you can hang out with skaters, it's where the alternative scene happens and it's all a little less chic. A little later, we moved on to the Korean district, where we sampled an awful lot of things: **pork and kimchi stir-fry** (buta kimchi) and **fried rice and noodles** (sobameshi), as well as typical Osaka dishes such as **sweet and sour pork** (subuta) and **Osaka-style savoury pancakes** (okonomiyaki).
The time came for me to say goodbye to my four colleagues. The next day, I was to travel on to Tokyo with Tomoko and Miho. My colleagues were to fly home. But not without one last culinary extravaganza. The five of us could barely fit inside the standing bar under the railway lines at Fukushima station, but we were lucky: sushi is only made there once a month, and apparently we had chosen the right evening. We visited the Umeda Sky Building, where we enjoyed a fabulous view over Osaka. It left my head spinning. We continued on to the Kyobashi district, in search of the legendary Toyo standing bar. What an incredible ambiance! We absorbed the atmosphere and fully immersed ourselves in the culinary bath of sushi and small snacks, including **crab and scallops with ponzu vinaigrette** (kani to hotate no ponzu gake). It was a mind-blowing, melt-in-the-mouth experience. On our way back, we stopped again at Namba Dotonburi. You've never seen anything like it in your life: an entertainment street stretching for miles, with clubs, dance halls, karaoke, bowling alleys, cinemas, and of course restaurants and street food.

I think we must have talked to about half the population of Osaka that evening, or so it seemed. The people of Osaka are very welcoming – just show an interest in food and they'll take you in tow. Eat 'till you drop really is an Osaka saying. We closed down many an eatery and almost died laughing until it was time to wend our way back to Tengachaya. Now and again, we stopped at a convenience store for a cool beer.

It wouldn't be much longer before we were back home again on the merry-go-round of a chef's life and back up to our eyes in kitchen stress. But in one way or another, that's precisely why you work in a restaurant. You work for each other. Together, you perform a chain of events with the shared goal of surprising your guests with a tasty and beautifully presented meal. The life of a chef is hard, but you do it for the camaraderie and the feeling of being in it together.

GYUNIKU NO TAMAGO-TOJI 牛肉の卵とじ
THINLY SLICED BEEF WITH EGG

The combination of egg, thinly sliced meat and dashi is very popular in Japan. The lightly beaten egg is usually added at the last minute, after which the heat is immediately turned off, so that the dish stays juicy. If you serve this dish over hot rice, it is a meal in itself: tanin-don.

480 ml (2 cups) dashi (see p. 196)

4 tablespoons soy sauce

4 tablespoons mirin

2 tablespoons sake

2 onions, in strips

200 g (8 ounces) thinly sliced beef (preferably entrecôte)

4 shiitake, in strips

4 eggs, lightly beaten

10 cm (4 inches) spring onion, in thin rings

Mix the dashi, soy sauce, mirin and sake in a bowl. First put the onions in the saucepan, then the meat and the shiitake. Carefully spoon the dashi over the ingredients. Bring everything to the boil over medium heat. Now work quickly: as soon as the meat is cooked, add half of the eggs. When the eggs have almost set, add the rest of the egg. Sprinkle with spring onion and quickly put the lid on the pan. Turn off the heat and leave to stand for 1 to 2 minutes. Spoon on to a plate or serve straight from the pan.

If you use chicken instead of beef, this make a different but equally delicious and popular dish: oyako-don (see "The shopping street: Tenjinbashisuji Shotengai" on p. 142).

THE SHOPPING STREET
TENJINBASHISUJI SHOTENGAI

Across from the house where I lived until I was seventeen there was a little shopping street. It had a coffee shop, an udon place, a sweet shop, a bakery, a Chinese restaurant, a sports shop, a *karate-dojo*, a barber shop, a dry cleaners, etc.. I often played on our drive with the children from the shopping street until closing time, which could be fairly late. I also went to the bakery regularly, not only to buy delicious cakes, but also just to play. I was always allowed to stay to see how they made the cakes and biscuits (such as the typical *castela*, a loan word from Portuguese, see recipe on p. 123). I learned how egg yolk was separated from the white, that the edges of the *castela* are in fact the tastiest part, etc.. I still remember the amazing smell upon entering the udon house, the specific smell of the dashi (stock), which was different in each restaurant. My favourite *tanin-don* (see recipe on p. 140). Just put it over hot rice in a *donburi* (bowl) and it's ready. *Tanin* means "strangers". So this dish is prepared with egg and beef, which are not in the same "family". *Oyako-don*, on the other hand, consists of egg and chicken, literally "parent and child". The same dashi was used for all dishes, which is why the taste of the dashi is representative of the restaurant itself and is therefore critically important.

There were other shopping streets within walking distance, where fresh ingredients such as fish, meat and vegetables could be purchased. In our neighbourhood, we also had a covered market, where I often went with my mother. Everyone there knew everyone else and sometimes all the chatting to acquaintances took longer than the actual shopping. As a snack, my mother always bought a deep-fried croquette for me from the butcher; it was a potato croquette with a bit of beef inside it. Those croquettes from the butcher were the best ever!

Tom, Luk, Miho and I visited Tenjinbashisuji, close to the famous Tenmangu temple. It is the longest shopping street in Japan. During the Edo period (1603-1868) Osaka was known as the "country's kitchen". Seventy percent of all goods in Japan were gathered and traded there. This prosperity was due to its geographical accessibility, the many canals and the harmonious relations between merchants and townspeople. In Osaka, merchants amassed considerable wealth and, consequently, power. The unique aspect of this was that they then used their money to build bridges and buildings and for culture and education. The townspeople wanted to build their city themselves and to ensure its success. Typical Osaka, so it was said.

During this Edo period, Tenjinbashisuji developed in the vicinity of the temple into one of the three largest markets for vegetables and fruit in Osaka and, since then, the district has played a crucial role. With centralisation focusing on a different market during the 1930s, the emergence of big new department stores and the development of public transport, Tenjinbashisuji ran into serious difficulties, but the merchants joined forces to survive as an appealing, friendly shopping street. Today it is still the most famous street in Osaka and offers good quality at attractive prices.

In Japan you'll find many shopping streets all over the country, for example, there is one beside almost every station. If you have the chance, you must definitely take a stroll down one of them. You will discover a small but authentic piece of Japanese culture.

GYU STEEKI WAFU-SOSU
牛ステーキ和風ソース
STEAK WITH JAPANESE SAVOURY SAUCE

Soy sauce goes surprisingly well with steak. Adding some savoury Japanese aromatics makes it taste even more delicious. You can serve the sauce at the table but, in this recipe, you are actually supposed to add the sauce to the pan while frying. This combines and intensifies the flavours of the meat and of the sauce.

4 steaks

SAUCE

¼ onion, grated

1 teaspoon garlic, grated

1 teaspoon ginger, grated

100 ml (½ cup) soy sauce

75 ml (⅓ cup) white balsamic vinegar

50 ml (¼ cup) vegetable oil

Mix all the sauce ingredients in a bowl. Heat the oil in a frying pan and fry the meat until crispy on both sides. Add 6 to 8 tablespoons of sauce. Simmer the meat and let the sauce thicken uncovered. Serve immediately with extra sauce in a separate bowl.

You can store the sauce for a long time in the refrigerator. If you leave the sauce to stand for one night, its flavour will be milder.

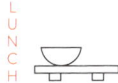

TSUMETAI RYOKUCHA
冷たい緑茶
COLD GREEN TEA

Shizuoka prefecture is known throughout Japan for its many high-quality tea fields. A good friend, who comes from this area, taught us the best way to make cold green tea. You brew the tea with cold water, which gives it a mild flavour and a pleasant green colour. Use a glass teapot so that the colour of the tea can shine on the dining table.

2 tablespoons Japanese green tea leaves

1 litre (1 quart) cold water

Put the tea leaves in a pot and pour on cold water. Mix with a spoon and leave overnight in the refrigerator. Stir now and again if possible. Remove the mixture from the refrigerator and mix well again with a spoon. Remove the tea leaves with a strainer and store the cold tea in the refrigerator until you want to serve it.

If you make the green tea with hot water and then cool it, it will be brownish in colour.

MATCHA KAKIGORI 抹茶かき氷
SHAVED ICE WITH GREEN TEA SYRUP

Kakigori can be found at every summer festival in Japan. Various types of syrup can be used. Matcha gives it a fresh, natural flavour.

SHAVED ICE

600 ml (3 cups) water

6 tablespoons sugar

condensed milk, if desired

SYRUP

1 tablespoon matcha powder (green tea powder)

6 tablespoons sugar

4 tablespoons water

Mix the water and sugar in a pan until the sugar has completely dissolved. Pour the sugar water into an ice cube tray and place in the freezer. In the meantime, make the syrup: mix the matcha powder, sugar and water in a microwave-safe bowl. Heat uncovered for 1 to 2 minutes in the microwave at 600 W. Cool in a cold water bath. Remove the ice cubes from the freezer and leave to stand for 5 minutes at room temperature. Put the ice cubes in a shaved ice machine and finely shave them. Make an iceberg in a bowl. Pour the syrup and condensed milk (if desired) over the iceberg. Serve with a spoon.

MASCARPONE NO MONAKA マスカルポーネの最中
MONAKA WITH MASCARPONE

8 thin, light and crispy wafer biscuits

160 g (6 ounces) mascarpone

1 teaspoon matcha powder (green tea powder)

100 g (4 ounces) sweetened adzuki beans (see p. 206)

Place four wafers on your work surface. Place a scoop of mascarpone (40 g (1 ½ ounces)) on each wafer. Sprinkle the mascarpone with the green tea powder. Divide the adzuki beans among the wafers in the same way. Now cover each wafer topped with mascarpone and adzuki beans with a "lid" made from the remaining crispy wafers.

OSAKA CHAKAI
TENJINBASHI 2-1-25-1F, KITA-KU, OSAKA 530-0041
OPEN DAILY: 9 AM – 11 PM

MATCHA LATTE 抹茶ラテ
JAPANESE GREEN TEA LATTE

Matcha is very popular, not only because it is tasty but also because of its nutritional value. It contains many positive ingredients and is, in a nutshell, very good for your appearance. The Japanese like the pure matcha flavour, but when mixed with milk it is also very popular. Its taste is bitter but at the same time sweet and creamy. Enjoy its complex flavour!

4 teaspoons matcha powder (green tea powder)

40 g (¼ cup) sugar

600 ml (3 cups) milk

Place the matcha powder and sugar in a large bowl. Heat the milk in a small saucepan until it is almost boiling. Gradually add the hot milk to the matcha mixture while gently beating it with a whisk. Make sure that the sugar dissolves completely. Divide into four cups. Add milk foam and matcha powder if desired.

KUNSEI TAMAGO 燻製卵
SMOKED EGGS

This dish seems complicated and does take quite a long time to prepare but the unique, deep flavour makes this appetiser more than worth the effort. The most difficult step is removing the egg shells from the soft-boiled eggs. All the remaining steps are easy and add additional complexity to this amazing taste explosion.

6 soft-boiled eggs
wood smoker chips

MARINADE

150 ml (⅔ cup) water
1 teaspoon salt
4 tablespoons soy sauce
1 tablespoon mirin

Carefully remove the egg shells in cold water. Combine all the marinade ingredients in a bowl. Put the peeled eggs in a freezer bag and add the marinade. Squeeze the air out of the bag and seal it. Leave the eggs to marinate overnight in the refrigerator. Remove the eggs from the marinade and dry with paper towel. Place the smoker chips in the smoking pan (or smoker) and start the smoking process. Add the eggs when the chips start to smoke and leave to smoke on a low heat for 15 to 30 minutes.

The eggs are also delicious just marinated, without smoking them.

MARKET STREET

24/7

NIKU KOROKKE 肉コロッケ
JAPANESE-STYLE CROQUETTES WITH MINCED MEAT

This is a very popular dish in Japan and is served as a meal with rice and vegetable salad. In order to fully appreciate the contrast in texture, you must eat this dish as soon as it has been fried so as to experience the crispy panko on the outside and the soft potato puree with minced meat inside.

vegetable oil

½ onion, finely chopped

150 g (4 ounces) minced meat (beef/pork)

2 tablespoons soy sauce

2 tablespoons sugar

500 g (1 pound) potatoes

50 ml (¼ cup) full-fat cream

salt

BATTER

flour

a few eggs, lightly beaten

panko (dry breadcrumbs)

Heat a dash of oil in a pan, add the onion and fry, then add the minced meat and stir-fry for a few minutes until golden brown. Add soy sauce and sugar and continue frying over a low heat. Stir regularly. Turn off the heat as soon as the cooking liquid has completely disappeared.

Boil the potatoes until cooked and mash to a puree. Add the cream and the minced meat. Mix well and season to taste with salt. Make croquettes to your preferred shape. Place three dishes containing flour, eggs and panko on the work surface. Roll each croquette first in the flour, then the egg and, finally, in the panko.

Heat the frying oil to 170 °C (340 °F) and fry the croquettes until golden brown. Drain on paper towel and serve immediately.

Just give this a try with tonkatsu sauce (see recipe p. 203)!

MARKET STREET

IZAKAYA

24/7

TONYU PURIN 豆乳プリン
SOY MILK PUDDING

The combination of the light soy flavour and the caramel sauce is delicious. It is even more tasty served cold.

2 eggs, lightly beaten
3 tablespoons sugar
400 ml (1 ½ cups) soy milk
boiling water

CARAMEL SAUCE
50 g (¼ cup) sugar
1 tablespoon cold water
2 tablespoons hot water

Mix together the sugar and cold water in a saucepan and place on the heat. Stir occasionally. Turn off the heat as soon as the caramel starts to turn nice and brown. Add the hot water but take care not to burn yourself. Stir again and set the caramel to one side.

Mix the eggs and sugar using a fork. Make sure that everything is mixed well but try not to create foam. Gradually add the soy milk and mix carefully. Strain the mixture and divide it among four small bowls. Place the bowls in a saucepan and pour boiling water into the pan to halfway up the bowls (au bain-marie). Cover the pan and cook for 7 minutes over a low heat. Turn off the heat and leave the bowls to stand in the hot water for 15 minutes. Remove them from the water and leave to cool. Cover the bowls and place in the refrigerator. Pour the caramel sauce over the pudding when it has thoroughly cooled and serve immediately.

You can add two tablespoons of cocoa powder for a chocolate flavour. Mix well before cooking.

OKURA TO TORINIKU NO SALADA
オクラと鶏肉のサラダ
OKRA AND CHICKEN SALAD

'Okra' may sound Japanese but it is in fact an English loan word. The vegetable came to Japan at the end of the nineteenth century and has become very popular especially since the 1950s. This salad has a creamy sesame vinaigrette that is delicious when combined with vegetables and chicken.

600 ml (3 cups) water

2 tablespoons sake

½ teaspoon salt

250 g (8 ounces) chicken fillet, in long strips

6 okra

½ cucumber, in chunks

1 tomato, in chunks

VINAIGRETTE

2 teaspoons grated ginger

2 tablespoons sesame paste

2 tablespoons sugar

2 tablespoons soy sauce

1 tablespoon miso

1 tablespoon white balsamic vinegar

Bring the water to the boil. Add sake, salt and the chicken strips. Turn off the heat as soon as the water boils again and leave the chicken to stand for 3 minutes in the cooking liquid. Remove the chicken strips from the cooking liquid and tear the meat by hand into smaller strips. Place the okra on a microwave-safe plate with a lid and heat them 2 to 3 minutes in the microwave at 600 W. Cut them into slices.

Combine all the vinaigrette ingredients in a bowl. Place the vegetables and meat in a dish. Spoon the sauce over and serve.

Select okra that are not too big, otherwise the fibres are hard to eat. When you cut okra they are sticky. This stickiness comes from the various fibres, and these are good for your cholesterol level.

OKURA TO
TORINIKU
NO SALADA
**OKRA AND
CHICKEN
SALAD**

NASU NO
ORANDANI
**EUROPEAN/
DUTCH-STYLE
AUBERGINES
SEE P. 161**

DASHIMAKI
TAMAGO
**JAPANESE
OMELETTE
SEE P. 162**

NASU NO ORANDANI
茄子のオランダ煮
EUROPEAN/DUTCH-STYLE AUBERGINES (EGGPLANT)

This recipe literally means "Dutch-style aubergines". In Japan, nobody is really sure that this recipe actually comes from the Netherlands but, in any event, the technique of deep-frying and then marinading came to Japan via European merchant ships. This technique allows vegetables to shine and gives them a rich flavour. Today, this dish can be found in the prepared food section of most supermarkets.

1 large aubergine, approximately 8-9 cm (3.5 inches) in diameter, cut into 3-cm (1 inch) chunks

1 tablespoon vegetable oil

1 teaspoon sesame oil

400 ml (1 ½ cups) dashi (see p. 196)

1 tablespoon sugar

1 ½ tablespoons soy sauce

2 tablespoons sake

1 teaspoon grated ginger

Place the aubergine chunks in a large bowl of cold water and leave for a few minutes. Drain them and pat dry with paper towel. Heat the vegetable oil and sesame oil in a pan, then fry the aubergine until it is semi-cooked. Soak up the oil in the pan with paper towel and then add the dashi, sugar, soy sauce and sake. Simmer for approximately 5 minutes until the aubergine chunks are soft. Leave to cool and place in the refrigerator. Garnish with grated ginger and serve cold. Makes a perfect dish for a hot day.

This dish is even more tasty if left overnight in the refrigerator.

MARKET STREET

DASHIMAKI TAMAGO 出し巻き卵
JAPANESE OMELETTE

Dashimaki tamago, or more commonly tamagoyaki, is a standard component of the typical Japanese bento box that is eaten cold at lunch time. But this Japanese omelette only tastes truly fantastic when it is freshly made! Juicy and hot, with the full flavour of the dashi, this simple dish is guaranteed to put a smile on your face. To begin with, it might be a little difficult to make it the right shape, but practice makes perfect and the results are worthy of a feast!

There are two types of omelette: sweet and non-sweet. Here, our recipe is for sweet dashimaki.

3 eggs
2 teaspoons sugar
½ teaspoon salt
40 ml (⅛ cup) dashi (see p. 196)
2 tablespoons vegetable oil

Beat the eggs, sugar, salt and dashi in a bowl. Heat a tablespoon of oil in a Japanese rectangular pan or a small frying pan over a medium heat. Add approximately half the egg mixture and tilt the pan to achieve an even coverage. When the egg starts to set but the top is still runny, roll up the omelette using a spatula from the top of the pan to the bottom. Move the omelette to the top of the pan and add a tablespoon of oil, followed by the remaining egg mixture. Lift up the rolled-up omelette and let the new egg mixture flow underneath the roll. Once it has set, roll the omelette again from top to bottom.

Place the omelette on a chopping board and leave to cool for 1 or 2 minutes. Cut into slices 1 cm (½ inch) thick and serve.

You can also mix finely chopped spring onions with the egg so that the omelette has a pretty green garnish, as well as an additional fresh taste.

MAEDA TOFU
TENJINBASHI 3-4-9,
KITA-KU, OSAKA 530-0041
OPEN: MON - SAT, 11 AM - 7 PM

IZAKAYA AND TACHINOMIYA

Delicious drinks and snacks, that's what the *Izakaya* and *tachinomiya* are all about – two typically Japanese "pubs". The place where the two main characters meet in the novel *The Briefcase*, by Hiromi Kawakami, is this type of small izakaya near the station, with delicious, house-made snacks to go with the sake. A retired Japanese teacher sees his former pupil, Tsukiko, for the first time in many years. She does not immediately recognise him but notices him when they order exactly the same dishes simultaneously while seated on their bar stools: tuna with *natto*, finely-chopped lotus root and salted shallots. This "local bar" is the ideal place for the two of them, who are alike in that they usually keep their distance from others, and yet in this case they seek a rapprochement through the drink and the snacks.

Etymologically speaking, izakaya 居酒屋 is a combination of two words: *izake* 居酒 (sake that you drink sitting down) and *sakaya* 酒屋 (the place where sake is made and sold). Nowadays, the word has become synonymous the world over with "bar with Japanese-style snacks". You could also compare it to a bar where you can taste many different kinds of (Japanese) tapas. *Tachinomiya* literally means a bar where you drink standing up. The Japan Anniversary Association even recognises a *tachinomi* day, 11 November. This date was chosen because the shape of 11/11 looks like people standing up. This style is perhaps ideally suited to large cities – it's a way of making a confined space as cosy as possible. At izakayas and tachinomiyas you can eat and drink with friends, colleagues or your partner. On weekdays you'll see many people wearing suits in an izakaya, who have come straight from work for a drink with their co-workers. A tachinomiya is usually much smaller than an izakaya and, as the name suggests, has no stools or chairs. You can even go to a tachinomiya on your own for a shot or a quick but tasty snack (even if you do ultimately stay much longer than planned). I used to have the impression that a tachinomiya was a place where only (older) men went to get drunk. But nowadays you also see a lot of women and students in them. In any event, they are lively places where you can enjoy cheap, tasty food and drinks.

A girlfriend of mine runs a liquor store in Osaka with her husband. She took over the shop from his parents. As well as the shop, they also have a small tachinomiya, where they also offer *oden* (see recipe, p. 83). Every day, they add new ingredients and seasonings to the special *oden* pot, but the surplus stock stays in the pot so that every day the stock takes on a richer flavour, which nobody can imitate. This is a characteristic tradition for a small tachinomiya.

HIJIKI GOHAN ひじきご飯
RICE WITH HIJIKI SEAWEED

Hijiki looks a bit odd but it does not have a strong flavour and is very nutritious and healthy. In old Japan, people believed that you would live a long life if you ate a lot of hijiki. Enjoy this nutritious ancient Japanese dish.

20 g (¼ cup) dried hijiki (seaweed)

600 ml (2 ½ cups) Japanese rice

½ carrot, in thin strips, 2-cm (1-inch) long

550 ml (1 pint) dashi (see p. 196)

4 tablespoons soy sauce

4 tablespoons mirin

toasted sesame seeds

Rinse the hijiki in cold water and soak in water for 30 minutes. Take it out of the water and remove any hard pieces.

Wash the rice five times or more until the water is almost clear. Leave the rice in cold water for 30 minutes. Then pour off the water and leave the rice to drain in a colander. You need an electric rice cooker for the next step. If you do not have an electric rice cooker, you can also use a pressure cooker that can hold at least three times the volume of the raw rice. Place the drained rice, the hijiki, carrot strips, dashi, soy sauce and mirin in the bowl of the electric rice cooker or into the pressure cooker and mix carefully. Close the rice cooker and start the cooking programme. If you are using a pressure cooker, close the lid and bring to the boil over high heat, until the pan is pressurised. Then leave to cook over a low heat for 5 minutes. Turn off the heat and leave to stand for 15 minutes. Cool the pressure cooker with cold water. Open the pressure cooker or rice cooker and break up the rice with a wooden spoon so as to introduce some air into it. Divide into the various serving bowls and garnish with sesame seeds.

Hijiki contains a lot of calcium, iron, magnesium, vitamin A and fibre. In brief: it's good for women!

SAKE NO SAIKYO YAKI
鮭の西京焼き
MISO-MARINATED AND BAKED SALMON

This dish comes from Kyoto, from where sweet saikyo miso also originates. The miso marinade expels the water from the fish and then impregnates it with the sweet taste of miso. While it is baking, take care not to let the fish overcook and especially not to burn it!

500 g (1 pound) salmon, cut into 4 pieces

Combine all the marinade ingredients in a bowl. Cover the fish with the marinade and leave to marinate in the refrigerator for 30 to 60 minutes.

MARINADE

4 tablespoons white miso
1 tablespoons sake
4 tablespoons mirin
2 ½ tablespoons sugar

In the meantime, preheat the oven to 180 °C (350 °F). Take the fish out of the marinade and carefully remove the marinade until only a thin layer remains on the fish. Bake the fish in the oven. Cover the fish with aluminium foil as soon as it is nicely browned but not yet completely cooked. Leave to cook for a few more minutes. Serve immediately.

This dish is also delicious made with cod or sea bream instead of salmon. You can also use this marinade for meat, such as pork chops, but in that case it is best to fry the meat in a pan rather than baking it in the oven.

BUTA KIMCHI 豚キムチ
PORK AND KIMCHI STIR-FRY

Kimchi (spicy fermented vegetables) may well come from Korea but the Japanese are crazy about it! Kimchi is delicious on its own but here it is used as a seasoning in another dish. The complex flavour of kimchi combines spicy, salty, sweet and the acidity of fermentation. Just put it in the wok with the pork – simple and above all delicious!

400 g (1 pound) unsalted pork, thinly sliced

1 onion, thinly sliced

1 teaspoon salt

2 teaspoons sugar

2 tablespoon sesame oil

black pepper to taste

1 tablespoon vegetable oil

200 g (8 ounces) Chinese cabbage kimchi

Place all the ingredients except the kimchi into a bowl and mix well using your hand. Leave to stand for 15 minutes.

Heat the oil in a pan and add the meat mixture. Stir-fry over medium heat. When the meat is almost ready, add the kimchi and fry a little longer. Serve with cooked rice.

Kimchi is available in endless varieties. For this dish, you can also use daikon or other vegetable kimchi. Kimchi can be found in Korean and Asian shops, or you can make it yourself using ready-made kimchi sauce.

SOBAMESHI そばめし
FRIED RICE AND NOODLES

Very useful dish if you happen to have yesterday's leftover rice.

80 g (3 ounces) noodles (ramen, Chinese rice noodles)

4 tablespoons vegetable oil

100 g (4 ounces) mixed minced meat (beef/pork)

2 tablespoons sake

½ onion, finely grated

1 small carrot, brunoise

60 g (2 ounces) Chinese cabbage, in long thin strips

180 g (6 ounces) cooked rice, preferably from the previous day (see p. 198)

4 tablespoons tonkatsu sauce (see p. 203)

2 spring onions in rings

Prepare the noodles according to the packet directions. Rinse under running water so that they do not stick together. Cut the noodles with scissors into 2-cm pieces. Set aside.

Heat two tablespoons of oil over a low heat in a wok. Fry the minced meat until cooked; at the end add the sake to taste. Remove from the wok. Add another two tablespoons of oil to the same pan and fry the onion and the carrot until glazed. Start with the onion and then add the carrot. Add the cabbage and stir until almost cooked. Return the minced meat to the pan and stir well. Add the noodles and the rice. Stir well again. Now add the tonkatsu sauce. Garnish with the spring onion.

Endless variations are possible, using different vegetables, meat, scampi or ... add kimchi for a touch of spice or bonito flakes for a more salty flavour.

If you leave out the rice, you have actually made yakisoba, which is also a really popular street food dish.

SUBUTA 酢豚
SWEET AND SOUR PORK

This dish originally comes from China but has since become a popular food in Japan. Everyone loves the combination of the salty meat with the sweet pineapple...

600 g (1.5 pounds) pork, diced into 3 cm (1 inch) pieces

2 tablespoons soy sauce

2 tablespoons sake

1 tablespoon sesame oil

1 carrot, in 1 cm (½ inch) pieces

1 onion, in 2 cm (1 inch) pieces

1 red or yellow pepper, in 2 cm (1 inch) pieces

2 tablespoons potato starch

¼ pineapple, in 2 cm (1 inch) pieces

SAUCE

6 tablespoons white balsamic vinegar

6 tablespoons soy sauce

4 tablespoons sugar

4 tablespoons ketchup

4 tablespoons sake

2 tablespoons mirin

8 tablespoons water

Mix pork, soy sauce, sake and sesame oil in a bowl. Leave to stand for 10 minutes, Place the carrots, onions and peppers in a microwave-safe dish with a lid and heat them for 3 minutes at 600 W. Combine all the sauce ingredients in a bowl. Add the potato starch to the marinaded pork and mix well.

Heat the frying oil to 170 °C (340 °F) and fry the pork until cooked and light brown in colour. Drain the meat on kitchen paper.

Combine the sauce, vegetables, pineapple and pork in a cold pan. Place the pan on the heat and cook for 3-4 minutes over medium heat. Stir regularly. Spoon onto a plate and serve as soon as the sauce has thickened.

Fresh pineapple can be replaced by tinned pineapple, but in that case use less sugar in the sauce.

OKONOMIYAKI (OSAKA-STYLE)

お好み焼き(大阪風)

SAVOURY JAPANESE PANCAKES WITH CABBAGE (OSAKA-STYLE)

In Japan, an okonomiyaki is fried on the teppan, a big stainless steel griddle, but you can also just use an ordinary frying pan. This recipe forms the basis for okonomiyaki, but let your culinary creativity have free reign and use other ingredients such as scampi, calamari, mussels, cheese, kimchi, etc.. Add whatever you feel like and really make this your signature dish.

350 g (2 cups) white cabbage, in pieces of 0.5 to 1 cm (¼ to ½ inch)

50 g (2 ounces) spring onions

200 g (8 ounces) unsalted bacon slices

DOUGH

6 tablespoons flour

4 tablespoons grated potato

4 tablespoons dashi (see p. 196)

2 eggs

TO GARNISH

tonkatsu sauce (see p. 203)

Japanese mayonnaise

aonori (very fine flakes of dried seaweed)

bonito flakes

Place all the dough ingredients in a bowl and mix with a whisk. Place a handful of cabbage and the spring onions in another bowl, add a ladle of dough and mix well.

Heat the teppanyaki or frying pan and pour the mixture on to the hot surface. Make it into a round shape, 2 to 3 cm (1 to 2 inches) high. Cover the cabbage mixture with the slices of bacon. Turn the pancake over when the underside is golden brown and fry approximately 5 minutes over medium heat. Do not press down on the top of the pancake so as to keep the okonomiyaki soft and fluffy.

Draw a zig-zag pattern on the surface of the pancake with the tonkatsu sauce. Turn the pancake through 90 degrees and do the same with the mayonnaise. To finish, sprinkle some aonori and a small handful of bonito flakes over the okonomiyaki. Serve immediately.

ZOUYA
TAMADE NISHI 2-7-10,
NISHINARI-KU, OSAKA 530-0017
OPEN: TUES · SAT, 5 PM - 11 PM
SUN & PUBLIC HOLIDAYS, 3 PM - 11 PM

KANI TO HOTATE NO PONZU GAKE
カニとホタテのポン酢がけ
CRAB AND SCALLOPS WITH PONZU (JAPANESE CITRUS SOY SAUCE)

This dish sounds very luxurious because of the crab and scallops but in fact it is a very casual dish, the kind of thing fishermen cook themselves on the boat. Simply prepared and served in copious quantities on a large platter: take the plunge and enjoy!

1 live crab, 1.5 to 2 kg (3-4 pounds)

8 scallops

2 x 3 litres (2 x 3 quarts) water (for boiling and for cooling)

2 x 90 g (2 x ⅓ cup) salt (for boiling and for cooling)

ice cubes

TO GARNISH

A handful of chives, in 3-cm (1-inch) pieces

ponzu (Japanese citrus soy sauce)

Place the live crab in cold water for 10 to 15 minutes to rinse. In the meantime, bring water to the boil in a large pan and add the salt. Let the water boil vigorously. Add the crab to the boiling water. Cook the crab with the back facing down so that the insides cook quickly and do not move towards the legs. Place a small, heat-resistant plate on top of the crab to keep it submerged. Boil for 15 to 20 minutes.

Mix cold water and salt in a large bowl. Add the ice cubes. Remove the crab from the boiling water and reserve the water. Place the crab in the ice-cold, salted water. Leave to cool for 10 to 15 minutes so that the crab meat is easier to remove. Remove the crab from the water and drain. Break the legs, the claws and the body of the crab and take out the crab meat.

Bring the crab cooking liquid back to the boil and add the scallops. Boil for 3 to 5 minutes. Remove the scallops from the cooking liquid and cool for 10 minutes in the cold, salted water. Add some ice cubes if necessary. Place the crab meat, the scallops and the chives in a bowl and pour over a generous amount of ponzu. Serve cold.

If you cannot get fresh crab, you can use pre-cooked crab, provided it is of high quality and the crab meat is pure, not seasoned.

TOYO
HIGASHINODAMACHI 3-2-26
MIYAKOJIMA-KU, OSAKA 534-0024
OPEN: TUES - SAT, 3.30 PM - 9 PM

TOKYO FOOD CRAWL

The next day, while my colleagues were on the plane home, I was dozing on the shinkansen from Osaka to Tokyo. So who was left? Tomoko, Miho and I. Our goal was five days in Tokyo and this time Miho would be our guide. She lived and worked there for fifteen years. So I lay sleeping on the shinkansen, happy that I could finally take a nap, when I was suddenly awoken by a Japanese man. That put me in a bad mood straight away; I'd finally found a moment when I could rest and that rest was being disturbed. But he pointed, "You have to look! Mount Fuji!" I had often heard about how legendary Mount Fuji is from a spiritual perspective, but seeing the mountain with my own eyes was truly something else altogether. The landscape is fairly flat and then suddenly the train passes by this snow-covered mountain! For a couple of minutes, I had a perfect view of Mount Fuji and, once Mount Fuji comes into view, then you know that you're about to arrive in Tokyo.

The first thing we did at Tokyo Station was to put our luggage into lockers. Tokyo Station is a city unto itself – it really does have everything. There are shopping malls, entertainment, eating places, etc.. You could eat something different every day of your life even if you just stayed there. Once our luggage was locked away, we stepped outside, where I noticed some trendy people drinking something green. Tomoko and Miho soon realised that this was a **green soy bean shake** (*edamame sheiku*). We reasoned that had to be healthy so we all went to buy a shake.

We then took the metro to Roppongi Hills, where we found a small street food market. It was a little touristy, but we had a robust **scampi burger** (*ebi katsu burger*). A little further on, Tomoko also found a delicious dish of **rice with sea bream sashimi and hot dashi** (*tai chazuke*). In the evening, we went to explore the Asakusa district, where we were staying. Miho took us to a miso shop, where I had honestly the best miso I've ever tasted. The shop was full of old barrels full of miso. Miso is such a fantastic condiment and I am just crazy about it. You couldn't really eat a meal there, so at Miho's recommendation we went to a legendary *onigiri* shop. There, a lady has been making **hand-rolled rice balls** (*sake no onigiri*) for sixty years. The flavours, the many types of filling, the crispy seaweed combined with the soft, warm rice and the salty filling – it's making my mouth water all over again! The place was also perfectly charming: the combination of the old shop and the wonderful lady were just mind-blowing. I will never forget how she confided in me that you have to put all your respect and love into making these rice balls.

Then it was off to a suburb right on the other side of Tokyo, called Kichijoji. In the Harmonica Yokocho neighbourhood of narrow lanes we found ourselves in a completely different world, somewhere on the fourth floor of a dilapidated building. In fact, to get there we first had to go through the boss's living room. He was an old man with a long beard, sitting on a tatami (mat), just like a Confucian philosopher. That building seemed to be a kind of wooden hut to which random storeys had been added. On the top floor, where we had to go, it was as if we were sitting in the man's dining room. But we ate very well there: **grilled mackerel with sea salt** (*saba no shioyaki*). Harmonica Yokocho and all its narrow lanes is a really great neighbourhood with a lot of standing bars and hardly any tourists.

We continued our food expedition into another district, Ebisu. We had barely left the station when we came across a kind of food hall with fifteen restaurants. In fact, you could call it "proper street food", Singapore-style. We were surrounded by small restaurants with an abundance of food. We tried several carts, with plenty of alcohol along the way. Later – and by then we were well and truly under the influence – we also grilled some delicious meat.

Some hours later, we did eventually take the train back to our hotel – but in the wrong direction! Thankfully, we were on the circular line, so we made it to our destination, but it took an hour longer than planned.

EDAMAME SHAKE 枝豆シェイク
GREEN SOY BEAN SHAKE

A power food to get you through the day, brimming with proteins and fibre.

250 g (8 ounces) green soy beans (edamame), frozen, beans only (without skin)

350 g (12 ounces) vanilla ice cream

350 ml (1 ½ cups) milk

2 tablespoons sugar

pinch of salt

Put the frozen edamame in a blender and grind them into a smooth paste. Add the ice cream and milk and mix with the edamame. Add sugar and a pinch of salt and serve ice-cold.

You can replace the milk with soy milk.

ZUNDA SARYO DAIMARU TOKYO
DAIMARU DEPARTMENT STORE
MARUNOUCHI 1-9-1, CHIYODA-KU
TOKIO 100-0005
OPEN: DAILY: 10 AM - 8 PM

EBIKATSU BURGER えびカツバーガー
SCAMPI BURGER

The unique aspect of this dish is the texture of the scampi burger... If it's made well, the outside will be crispy and will contrast sharply with the fresh, juicy inside. Served in a soft burger bun with fresh lettuce, this creates not only a tasty but also a "texturally" surprising dish.

FILLING

30 medium scampi, in 5 mm (¼ inch) pieces

1 clove garlic, grated

2 tablespoons Japanese mayonnaise

1 tablespoon flour

2 tablespoons potato starch

1 tablespoon parsley, finely-chopped

salt and pepper

FOR BREADING

flour

a few eggs, lightly beaten

panko

TO FINISH

4 hamburger buns

tartar sauce

a few leaves of green lettuce

Combine all the filling ingredients in a bowl. Shape the filling into discs about 1-2 cm (½ – 1 inch) thick and 5 cm (2 inches) in diameter. Place flour, lightly beaten egg and panko on three separate dishes. Roll each burger first in the flour, then in the eggs and lastly in the panko.

Pour about 1 cm (½ inch) of oil into a frying pan and place on the heat. Put the burgers carefully into the oil and fry until crispy. Turn the burgers and fry until golden brown. Leave to drain on paper towel.

Spread tartar sauce on each bun. Put some lettuce on the bun and then the fried scampi burger. Top with the other half of the bun and serve.

TAI CHAZUKE 鯛茶漬け
RICE WITH SEA BREAM SASHIMI AND HOT DASHI

In traditional chazuke, hot Japanese tea is poured over cooked rice. This recipe is a more luxurious version of chazuke, in which sashimi is placed on top of the rice and dashi, rather than green tea, is poured over everything.

250 g (8 ounce) fillet of gilthead sea bream (dorade royal), skinless and boneless

4 small bowls cooked rice (see p. 198)

800 ml (3 cups) dashi (see p. 196)

MARINADE

2 teaspoons ginger, grated

4 tablespoons soy sauce

4 tablespoons mirin

4 tablespoons sake

2 tablespoons sugar

4 tablespoons sesame seeds, toasted

TO GARNISH

2 x 10 cm (1 x 5 inches) nori leaf, in strips of 3 mm x 2 cm (⅛ inch x 1 inch)

Combine all the marinade ingredients in a bowl. Cut the fish into slices of approximately 5 mm (¼ inch) thick and mix with the marinade. Leave to marinate in the refrigerator for 30 minutes.

Heat the rice in a covered bowl in the microwave oven and divide it among four small bowls. Take the fish out of the refrigerator and divide it among the bowls. Sprinkle the nori strips over the fish.

Heat the dashi in a pan. Pour the stock carefully over the rice and serve immediately.

SAKE NO ONIGIRI 鮭のおにぎり
HAND-ROLLED RICE BALLS WITH SALMON

Onigiri is everywhere in Japan, at every station and convenience store and in every imaginable variation. At the same time, however, everyone in Japan is convinced that the tastiest onigiri is the one that his or her mother made... That same mother passed on her love for her children by making the onigiri with her own hands. So challenge yourself to prepare your own onigiri with tenderness and love.

400 g (1 pound) skinless salmon fillet

salt

4 cups hot, cooked rice (see p. 198)

nori sheets, in 6 x 12 cm (3 x 6 inch) strips

Preheat the oven on grill setting. Place the salmon on a baking tray and sprinkle well with salt. Bake in the oven until the salmon is cooked. Remove the salmon from the oven and place in a bowl. Use a fork to break the salmon up into small pieces and then leave to cool. Remove any bones.

Place a bowl of water and a bowl of salt on the kitchen work top. Wet your hands with a little water and then dust with a little salt. Scoop up the rice with your hand (approximately the volume of a coffee cup) and make an indent in the middle. Press 2 or 3 teaspoons of salmon inside the rice and then mould the rice around the salmon into a ball. Shape the rice ball into a triangular shape with your hands by folding in half and then cross them and push together. Wrap with nori strips and serve.

The options for onigiri fillings are endless. Feel free to replace the salmon with tinned tuna mixed with some mayonnaise or salmon roe, fried chicken, scampi tempura, etc..

ONIGIRI ASAKUSA YADOROKU
ASAKUSA 3-9-10, TAITO-KU, TOKIO 111-0032
OPEN: 11.30 AM - 5 PM, EXCEPT SUNDAY
6 PM - 2 PM, EXCEPT WEDNESDAY

SABA NO SHIOYAKI 鯖の塩焼き
GRILLED MACKEREL WITH SEA SALT

This dish is also so popular in Japan that you'll see it everywhere: in bento boxes, in an izakaya restaurant or just at home as an everyday meal. In this simple dish, the combination of grilled mackerel, grated daikon and soy sauce produces a fresh and robust taste experience.

4 mackerel fillets

salt

sake

5 cm (2 inches) daikon (white winter radish) grated and squeezed dry

1 tablespoon soy sauce

Preheat the oven on grill setting. Using a sharp knife, make a few shallow incisions into the skin of the fish so that it keeps its nice fillet shape when grilled. Sprinkle both sides of the fish with salt and leave to stand for 10 minutes. Rinse the fish with some sake and dry with paper towel. Sprinkle the fish with a very small amount of salt and grill it in the oven until the skin colours a little and becomes crispy. Serve the mackerel hot, garnished with radish and soy sauce.

Other types of fish can be used instead of mackerel, such as bass, sea bream or sardines.

1 CHOME 1 BANCHI
KICHIJOJI HONCHO 1-1-1
MUSASHINO-SHI, TOKIO 180-0004
OPEN: MON - FRI, NOON - MIDNIGHT

A CHEF'S TABLE

The modern part of Tokyo was on the schedule for this day. We started in central Tokyo, or Ginza, in a real food truck area around Yurakucho station. A very international crowd comes to eat lunch there at midday, so you can find Thai, Argentine and Mexican food. We tried **rice bowl with salsa** (*salsa sosu no karaage don*), after which we ambled a bit more through the neighbourhood and waited for the end of the working day. As you have already learned from our wanderings around *izakayas* and standing bars, street food in Japan only really gets going "after hours".

One metro stop past Yurakucho is the district of Shinbashi, south of the Imperial Palace Grounds. The royal palace is not open to the public, but you can visit the gardens. To my mind, this neighbourhood exudes the true ambiance of Tokyo: a cluster of small restaurants and standing bars crammed under the railway line, where office workers take a break after the working day and before taking the train home (tip: ask for the Gado Shita neighbourhood).

And then our last evening came around. No visit to Tokyo is complete without exploring the districts of Shinjuku and Shibuya. Shinjuku has the busiest metro station in the world: four million passengers pass through it every day. Nonetheless, people do not bump into each other and everything actually runs very smoothly. Following a splendid panoramic view and a much over-priced drink at the Park Hyatt Hotel – yes, the hotel where Scarlett Johansson and Bill Murray met in the film *Lost in Translation* – we took a stroll down Memory Lane, a neighbourhood just a few alleyways in width, but known for its street food. Tourists know the way there, but the atmosphere is still warm and welcoming.

"Let's go wild in Shibuya!" I cried, turning to the guide. Shibuya is the neighbourhood for young, trendy people. Near the station we again found ourselves in a narrow street with tiny bars that could barely hold five people. One of the owners was just hanging out his *noren* (Japanese curtain) to show that the bar was opening. He gave us a warm welcome, we hung our jackets on the hooks, Miho and Tomoko placed their handbags in the baskets provided under the counter for that purpose. There was no menu: you ate whatever the chef was making. You could order something but whether you would actually get that thing on your plate depended on having the ingredients in stock.

We started with pieces of toast with potato and sprats, burrata with daikon and snacks made from sticky rice and blue cheese (*mochi*). It was a lucky shot, but we struck gold: it was genuine fusion cuisine at its best! And yet another example of a typically stylish little Japanese world. Anyway, more people came into the restaurant and we were all introduced to one another. We ordered more *shochu* and the owner – who by then we were calling Shefu – allowed us to sample his preserved plums. Every year he makes them himself, he told us, "It's all about getting the right salt ratio for pickling the plums". In the meantime, I put Tomoko's language lessons into practice. We got to know a couple of guys from Tokyo's ice hockey team, exchanged business cards with them, and had fun with the other guests. Every time someone asked for "*o kanjo*" (the bill), more diners came to take their places and I chatted to them too.

We *kampai*-ed with every swig from our glasses. Suddenly, in my somewhat tipsy state, I had a bright idea. I told the owner that back home in Ghent, Belgium, I had a ramen bar. The entire room lapsed into disbelief, with "ooohs" and "aaahs" swirling around my head. So I got out my iPad and showed them my web page. I was showered with admiration and the Shefu immediately invited me behind the bar to make ramen

with him. I hesitated at first, but I didn't want to disappoint the other customers, plus of course I had something to prove.

With my friend Shefu, I eventually made eight portions of ramen using what we found in the store cupboard: oxtail stock and a simple topping of bacon bits, spring onions and marinated bamboo shoots (*menma*). Tomoko and Miho served the portions to the other guests. I'm still not sure how we eventually managed to get away from that bar. What I do still remember are the friendly farewells from all those special people we had got to know. Tomoko left her mobile behind in the bar but we soon got it back. In the metro, somebody tapped her on the shoulder and said, "Here's your phone". Again, such politeness is typical of Japan.

Even when I was back home in Ghent, I was still glowing from that amazing evening, remembering the owner and me, together at the stove in Shibuya, Tokyo. We did a good job of improvising a fine ramen creation. One of the best moments of this entire voyage of discovery – and of this book – was the izakaya evening that Tomoko, Miho and Laurens organised at Ramen in Ghent a few months after we got home. One booking had been cancelled that evening, so I went as a guest myself. Honestly, that evening I tasted the best Japanese food I have ever had in Belgium. It all came flooding back to me: images of our crazy train journeys, our insane food crawls, the warm atmosphere of the izakayas and standing bars we had visited and, in particular, the love and passion of craftsmen or *shokunin* for their product, preparation or dish.

SALSA SOSU NO KARAAGE DON
サルサソースの唐揚げ丼
KARAAGE-DON (RICE BOWL) WITH SALSA

This dish is a variation on the fried chicken mentioned on p. 55 of this book. The combination with tomato salsa gives this dish a fresh, spicy taste. Delicious on a hot day!

4 bowls of cooked rice (see p. 198)

20 pieces of fried chicken (see p. 55)

SALSA

1 tomato, finely diced

½ small onion, finely chopped

½ red pepper, finely chopped

6 tablespoons ketchup

1 tablespoon lemon juice

Tabasco to taste

⅓ teaspoon salt

black pepper to taste

few springs of parsley, finely chopped

Mix all the salsa ingredients in a bowl and leave to stand for 30 minutes. Scoop the hot rice into a bowl and place the hot fried chicken on the rice. Scoop the salsa over the chicken and serve.

THE BASICS

DASHI
だし
JAPANESE STOCK

Dashi is the basis for many dishes. The special fragrance and its umami form the heart of Japanese cuisine. Thanks to the umami of dashi, less salt can be used. Various types exist, but the following three are the most common types of stock in Japan: kombu dashi (with dried seaweed), katsuo dashi (with katsuobushi, dried bonito flakes) and shiitake dashi (with dried shiitake).

KOMBU-DASHI

Kombu dashi is suitable for dishes where the taste and the fragrance of the ingredients take pride of place. The taste of the kombu dashi is not dominant or overwhelming, but plays a supporting role. It adds the umami to the ingredients. The component for the umami of the kombu is glutamic acid.

RECIPE WITH COLD WATER

500 ml (2 cups) water

10 g kombu (seaweed)

Gently clean the kombu with a well wrung-out cloth. Put the kombu in a covered pan with water and leave in a cool place for 10 hours.

RECIPE WITH HOT WATER

500 ml (2 cups) water

5 g kombu (seaweed)

Gently clean the kombu with a well wrung-out cloth.

Put the kombu in a pan with water. After 30 to 60 minutes, place over medium heat. Remove the kombu before the water starts to boil. If it is boiled for too long, its pleasant fragrance is lost.

KATSUO-DASHI

Katsuo dashi is used for dishes in which the stock plays a central role, such as sauce for cold noodles or (miso) soup. In fact, this is the most commonly used dashi in the Japanese family kitchen. It is delicious in combination with pork. The component for the umami of the katsuo dashi is inosinic acid.

500 ml (2 cups) water

20 g bonito flakes

Boil the water in a saucepan. When the water boils, add the bonito flakes. Turn down the heat to very low and cook for another 2 to 3 minutes. Turn off the heat. Strain the dashi (for clear dashi, use a tea towel or paper towel).

KOMBU- AND BONITO-DASHI

Kombu and bonito are often combined. This produces a deeper umami. For this the ingredients are:

1 litre (1 quart) water

10 g kombu (seaweed)

10 g bonito flakes

First follow the recipe with hot water for kombu dashi, then the recipe for katsuo dashi.

SHIITAKEDASHI

Shiitake dashi is used for dishes requiring a significant additional flavour from the taste and the fragrance of dried shiitake, for example sauce for cold noodles, wok dishes, soup, etc.. Dried shiitake has a stronger flavour, fragrance and umami than non-dried. The component for the umami of dried shiitake is guanosine monophosphate (guanylic acid), which is reinforced by its preparation.

15-25 g dried shiitake

500 ml (2 cups) cold water (preferably 0 °C (32 °F))

Soak the shiitake in water for 10 minutes. Wash them well with water. Put the shiitake in a covered pan with cold water and leave in the refrigerator for at least 24 hours. Remove the shiitake from the water and bring the water to the boil in a saucepan (for a clear dashi, strain the water before boiling using a tea towel or paper towel). When the water boils, remove the scum with a fine sieve and turn off the heat.

The shiitake can then be finely ground and cooked into dishes.

HAKUMAI
白米
COOKED RICE

600 ml (2 ½ cups) Japanese rice

600 ml (2 ½ cups) water

Wash the rice in a little water by gently swilling it around with the ball of your thumb without breaking the rice. Pour off the water and repeat this at least five times, until the water is almost clear. Leave the rice to stand for 30 minutes in cold water. Pour off the water and leave the rice to drain in a colander.

ELECTRIC RICE COOKER

Place the drained rice in the bowl of the electric rice cooker. Add the water but pay attention to the markings on the bowl. Depending on the type of rice cooker, the amount of water may differ from the amount given above. Close the rice cooker and start the cooking programme. Open the rice cooker and break up the rice with a wooden spatula to introduce some air into it.

PRESSURE COOKER

If using a pressure cooker, make sure that it can hold at least three times the volume of the uncooked rice. Put the drained rice and water into the pressure cooker. Cover with the lid and bring to the boil over high heat, until the pressure cooker is pressurised. Then leave to boil for another 5 minutes on low heat. Remove from the heat and leave to stand for 15 minutes. Cool the pressure cooker with cold water. Open the pressure cooker and break up the rice with a wooden spatula to introduce some air into it.

SAUCEPAN

If you want to use an ordinary saucepan, choose one with a thick base. Put the drained rice and water into the pan. Cover with the lid and place on a high heat. When it starts to boil, turn down the heat to low and boil for 12 minutes. Turn off the heat and leave to stand for 10 minutes. Remove the lid and break up the rice with a wooden spatula to introduce some air into it.

SUSHI MESHI
寿司飯
SUSHI RICE

This recipe makes approximately six small bowls of sushi rice.

SUSHI VINEGAR

5 tablespoons rice vinegar

4 tablespoons sugar

2 teaspoons salt

600 ml (2 ½ cups) Japanese rice

600 ml (2 ½ cups) water

kombu (seaweed), piece measuring approx. 8 x 8 cm (3 x 3 inches)

1 tablespoon sake

To make the sushi vinegar, combine the rice vinegar, sugar and salt in a bowl. Make sure that the sugar and the salt dissolve completely.

Wash the rice as described for plain cooked rice (see basic recipe on the previous page). Then place the drained rice with the water, kombu and sake in the rice cooker, pressure cooker or saucepan and follow the instructions for cooked rice.

When the rice is cooked, remove the kombu. Transfer the rice into a large, shallow bowl. Add the sushi vinegar gradually to the rice. Moisten a wooden spatula and use it to mix the rice. The rice will be sticky but try not to beat it because this will break the grains of rice. Turn the rice from bottom to top to separate it.

While turning, you can use a fan to cool the rice more quickly. This will produce attractive, shiny sushi rice. Dampen a tea towel and wring out the water. Cover the sushi rice with the towel and store it at room temperature until needed.

If you put the cooked sushi rice in the refrigerator, it will become hard and difficult to shape into individual sushi. You can heat up the rice briefly in the microwave in order to make it easy to manipulate again.

KATSUOBUSHI-JIO 鰹節塩
KATSUOBUSHI SALT

10 g bonito flakes

10 g coarse sea salt

Toast the bonito flakes gently in the oven for 10 minutes. Leave to cool and grind finely in a food mixer, together with the sea salt.

TORIGARA SOUP
鶏がらスープ
CHICKEN STOCK

2 whole chickens

2 kg (4.4 pounds) chicken carcasses

1 large piece kombu, cut sideways

100 g (4 ounces) dried shiitake, finely ground

kombu (seaweed)

3 cm (1 inch) ginger, crushed and grilled

1 large onion, halved and grilled

10 l (10 quarts) water

Add the kombu to the water and heat the water to 60 °C (140 °F). Leave to stand for one hour. Remove the kombu. Rinse the chickens and the carcasses under cold water.

Add the ground shiitake, ginger and onion to the water and bring to the boil. Add the chickens and carcasses and keep them at boiling point over the lowest possible heat. Skim regularly.

Simmer for 6 hours and strain through a towel. After 2 hours, break apart the whole chicken. Add (hot) water occasionally to maintain the same quantity of stock. Scrape off fat the next day. Keep the fat separately to give additional flavour to ramen dishes.

VEGE RAMEN NO SOUP
ベジラーメンのスープ
VEGETARIAN RAMEN STOCK

3 tablespoons butter

2 giant onions, coarsely chopped

4 leeks, cleaned and finely chopped

½ celeriac, chopped

1 fennel bulb, chopped

100 g (4 ounces) dried shiitake

400 g (14 ounce) can tomatoes

500 ml (2 cups) sake

bouquet garni (stalks of parsley, laurel and a couple of sprigs of thyme)

1 teaspoon pepper

1 tablespoon salt

Heat a large saucepan and melt the butter. Add the vegetables and stir well. Stew the vegetables for 15 minutes. Stir well from time to time. Add the shiitake and the tomatoes. Then soak with with sake. Let the alcohol evaporate. Cover with water and bring slowly to the boil. Add the bouquet garni, salt and pepper.

Just like at Tom's Ramen noodle bar!

TAMAGO NO SHOYUZUKE
卵の醤油漬け
EGGS IN SOY SAUCE

4 eggs
150 ml (⅔ cup) soy sauce
1 tablespoon sugar
75 ml (⅓ cup) mirin

Boil the eggs for 5 minutes. Remove from the cooking liquid and cool immediately in an ice bath. Cool the eggs for 15 minutes and peel them.

Combine the other ingredients and place the eggs in the mixture. Allow them to absorb the flavours for at least 2 hours.

MENMA メンマ
MARINATED BAMBOO SHOOTS

750 ml (3 cups) water
30 g (1 ounce) bonito flakes
50 ml (¼ cup) soy sauce
100 ml (½ cup) sake
40 ml (⅕ cup) mirin
20 g sugar
1 can sliced bamboo shoots (drained and rinsed)

Heat the water and add the bonito flakes. Bring just to the boil and then remove from the heat. Leave to stand for 30 minutes, strain the water and set aside. Add soy sauce, sake, mirin and sugar and allow to reduce (15 minutes). Add the bamboo shoots and simmer for 10 minutes.

GYOZA NO TARE 餃子のたれ
GYOZA DIPPING SAUCE

100 ml (½ cup) soy sauce
50 ml (¼ cup) rice vinegar
1 tablespoon chile oil

Mix all the ingredients together.

CHASHU チャーシュー
MARINATED BRAISED PORK

1 kg pork, preferably boneless

oil or butter

MARINADE

120 ml (½ cup) soy sauce

240 ml (1 cup) sake

240 ml (1 cup) mirin

64 g (⅓ cup) sugar

8 spring onions, roughly chopped

6 cloves of garlic, pressed

6 cm (2 inches) ginger, roughly chopped

1 shallot, roughly chopped

Combine all ingredients, heat, thicken and reduce.

Heat the oven to 80 °C (175 °F). Cut the meat into large slices, 20 x 8 cm (8 x 3 inches). Roll up the pieces and tie with string. Put the marinade in a casserole dish and place the meat in it. Cover with aluminium foil. After 2 ½ hours, check whether the meat is cooked. It should not be entirely hard. Allow the meat to cool.

Put a small amount of oil or butter in a pan and briefly fry the meat all over.

SHIITAKE AONORI BUTTER
椎茸青のりバター
SHIITAKE-SEAWEED BUTTER

10 g dried shiitake

100 g butter

1 tablespoon aonori (green seaweed powder)

In a food mixer, grind the shiitake into a fine powder. Melt the butter in a saucepan until it begins to foam slightly. Add the shiitake to the butter and simmer a few minutes. Remove from the heat and add the aonori. Stir well and leave to cool and set.

TONKATSU-SOSU
とんかつソース
TONKATSU SAUCE

2 tablespoons Worcestershire sauce

1 tablespoon oyster sauce

1 tablespoons ketchup

1 teaspoon soy sauce

1 teaspoon sugar

Place the ingredients in a mixing bowl and combine well using a mixer or whisk.

SHIODARE
塩だれ
CONCENTRATED SALT SAUCE

50 g sea salt or Himalaya salt

350 ml (1 ½ cups) water

4 onions, shredded

5 garlic cloves, crushed

3 cm (1 inch) ginger, finely chopped

Bring all the ingredients to the boil in a saucepan and reduce for 10 minutes.

MISODARE
味噌だれ
CONCENTRATED MISO SAUCE

½ cup miso paste

¼ cup sake

3 tablespoons mirin

20 g (1 ounce) ginger

1 teaspoon Japanese pepper

2 garlic cloves, crushed

Combine all ingredients, heat, thicken and reduce.

TANTANDARE
坦坦だれ
CONCENTRATED TANTAN SAUCE

2 tablespoons sesame paste

2 tablespoons tobanjan

1 cup chicken stock (see p. 200)

¼ cup soy sauce

20 g ginger

1 teaspoon salt

2 clove garlic, crushed

Combine all ingredients, heat, thicken and reduce.

BASILDARE
バジルだれ
CONCENTRATED PESTO SAUCE

½ clove of garlic

½ teaspoon sea salt

basil leaves from approximately 1 plant

60 g (⅓ cup) pine nuts, lightly toasted

60 g (⅔ cup) Parmesan cheese, grated

olive oil

finely ground black pepper

Finely crush the garlic and salt with a pestle and mortar. Add the basil and crush. Add the pine nuts and crush. Add Parmesan cheese and crush. Add a splash of olive oil to achieve the desired consistency. Season with pepper.

This is not really a dare, but we'll call it that for convenience.

TSUBUAN
つぶあん

SWEETENED ADZUKI BEANS

Japan does not really have a dessert culture, although sweet treats are often served with tea. One of the most popular ingredients of these treats is tsubuan. These sweetened adzuki beans are used as a filling for rice cakes or buns, but you can also just serve them with vanilla ice cream. They're very easy! Combined with matcha (green tea powder), they make a dish that is not only very traditional, but also especially tasty. Enjoy one of the most authentic of Japanese sweets.

300 g (10 ounces) dried adzuki beans

240 g (1 ⅓ cups) sugar

⅓ teaspoon salt

½ teaspoon soy sauce

Wash the adzuki beans and soak them in water for at least 8 hours.

Drain the adzuki beans and then pour them into a large pan. Add water and place the pan on the heat. Boil for 1 minute and then pour off the water. Add fresh water and bring to the boil again. Boil for another 1 minute and pour off the water. Wash the adzuki beans again and pour them back into the same pan. Add 1.2 litres (2 ½ pints) water and bring to the boil. Turn down the heat to low as soon as the water begins to boil and simmer the beans for approximately 2 hours. Make sure that the beans are always immersed in the water. Add water if necessary. Check whether the adzuki beans are ready. This will be when the skin of the beans is edible (not hard). If not ready, leave them to simmer a little longer.

Strain the adzuki beans but reserve the cooking liquid. Put the adzuki beans back into the same pan and add the sugar. Place over a low heat. Mix the beans and the sugar using a wooden spatula and make particularly sure that the beans at the bottom of the pan are stirred sufficiently, so that they cannot burn and stick to the pan. Add the salt and the soy sauce when the beans start to get heavier. Mix well and turn off the heat. If the beans are still a little too hard, add a small amount of the cooking liquid to soften them.

The beans are boiled briefly twice and then rinsed in order to eliminate the bitter, sharp taste and, in particular, to make their flavour milder.

DAIFUKU
大福

RICE CAKE FILLED WITH SWEETENED ADZUKI BEANS

Just the name itself is appealing. Literally, daifuku means "great luck". This traditional Japanese confection has many varieties nowadays, with strawberry, chestnut, plum, etc.. It is so soft – like a baby's skin – that everyone just wants to take a bite, which makes daifuku one of the most popular confections in Japan.

100 g (4 ounces) shiratamako (glutinous rice flour)

20 g sugar

150 g (⅔ cup) water

potato starch (to shape the batter discs)

180 g (7 ounces) sweetened adzuki beans (basic recipe on the previous page)

Mix shiratamako, sugar and water in a microwave-safe dish. Cook for 3 minutes in the microwave at 500 W, covered. Rinse a spatula in water and mix the dough until it is semi-transparent.

Sprinkle sufficient potato starch on the work surface to completely cover it and place the dough on it. Also sprinkle some potato starch over the dough. Cut the dough into six pieces using a knife. Sprinkle potato starch on your hand and flatten each piece of dough into a disc approximately 8 to 10 cm (3 to 4 inches) in diameter.

Place approximately one tablespoon of adzuki beans in the centre of the dough. Fold the dough over the beans and pinch the edges together. Shape the dough into a nice round cake and put it on a plate, coated with potato starch.

THE JAPANESE LANGUAGE

Linguistically speaking, Japanese is not related to the European languages, but it contains many loan words from English, as well as some from Dutch. The latter date from the seventeenth century until the mid-nineteenth century, when Japan was a closed country and the Netherlands was the only European country with which Japan had trade relations. However, the pronunciation of these loan words has been "Japonicised", i.e. "visitor" becomes "bijitaa". So you can try to pronounce English words in "Japanese style", but success is by no means guaranteed.

Many people understand basic English, particularly young people (generally speaking, the Japanese learn English for six years in secondary school), but even though they do their best to be helpful, speaking fluently remains a problem for many.

Nowadays, many signs are written in English (or at least in our alphabet), such as station information screens or signposts in major towns and cities. Ticket vending machines also show the names of stations using the Latin alphabet, so it's easy for you to find out how much you have to pay to get to a certain station.

As a tourist, being able to speak a few words of Japanese can certainly help break the ice and will please your Japanese acquaintances. Luckily, pronunciation is not too difficult and, particularly when you're enjoying a good meal, some short phrases can make people laugh!

ENGLISH	Phonetic Japanese	JAPANESE
Thank you	Arigato	ありがとう
You're welcome	Do itashimashite	どう致しまして
Good morning	Ohayo	おはよう
Hello	Konnichi wa	こんにちは
Good evening	Konban wa (Only as hello, not as goodbye)	こんばんは
Goodbye	Sayonara	さようなら
Bon appetit	Itadakimasu (Only when you yourself start eating)	いただきます
Thank you for the meal	Gochisosama deshita (When you have finished eating)	ごちそうさまでした
Cheers	Kanpai	乾杯
Tasty	Oishii	美味しい
Difficult	Muzukashii	難しい
It's OK	Daijobu desu	大丈夫です
I understand	Wakarimashita	分かりました
I don't understand	Wakarimasen	分かりません
This	Kore	これ
That	Sore (close to the person) / Are (further away)	それ あれ
Where is…?	… wa doko desu ka?	…はどこですか
How much does it cost?	Ikura desu ka?	いくらですか
I would like… (to eat)	… o kudasai	…をください
I like…	… ga suki desu	…が好きです

TOKIO

Edamame shake
ZUNDA SARYO DAIMARU TOKYO
Daimaru department store, Marunouchi 1-9-1,
Chiyoda-ku, Tokio 100-0005
Station: Tokio (Train: JR Yamanote line,
JR Chuo line and JR Keihin-Tohoku line)
Open daily: 10 am – 8 pm

Ramen
TOKIO RAMEN STREET
Marunouchi 1-9-1, Chiyoda-ku,
Tokio 100-0005
Station: Tokio (Train: JR Yamanote line,
JR Chuo line and JR Keihin-Tohoku line)
Open daily: 11 am – 11.30 pm

Ramen
AFURI
Ebisu 1-1-7, Shibuya-ku, Tokio 150-0013
Station: Ebisu (Train: JR Yamanote line,
JR Saikyo line and JR Syonanshinjuku line)
Open daily: 11 am – 5 pm

Hand-rolled rice balls (onigiri)
ONIGIRI ASAKUSA YADOROKU
Asakusa 3-9-10, Taito-ku, Tokio 111-0032
Station: Asakusa (Train: Tsukuba express
and Tobu-Isesaki line, Metro: Ginza line)
Open: 11.30 am – 5 pm except Sundays
6 pm – 2 am except Wednesdays

Grilled mackerel with sea salt
1 CHOME 1 BANCHI
Kichijoji honcho 1-1-1, Musashino-shi,
Tokio 180-0004
Station: Kichijoji (Train: JR Chuo line
and JR Somu line)
Open: Mon-Fri, noon – midnight

Station bento (ekiben)
EKIBEN MATSURI
Marunouchi 1-9-1, Chiyoda-ku,
Tokio 100-0005
Station: Tokio (Train: JR Yamanote line,
JR Chuo line and JR Keihin-Tohoku line)
Open daily: 5.30 am – 11 pm

Soba noodles
OWARIYA
Asakusa 1-7-1, Taito-ku, Tokio 111-0032
Station: Asakusa (Metro: Ginza line and
Tobu-Isesaki line)
Open: 11.30 am – 8.30 pm

Cake with sweetened adzuki beans (taiyaki)
NARUTO TAIYAKI HONPO
Asakusabashi 1-9-1, Taito-ku, Tokio 111-0053
Station: Asakusabashi
(Train: JR Chuo line and JR Somu line)
Open daily: 10 am - 10 pm

Octopus balls (takoyaki)
GANKOTAKO
Meguro 3-11-6, Meguro-ku, Tokio 153-0063
Station: Meguro (Train: JR Yamanote line,
Metro: Nanboku line and Mita line)
Open daily: 11 am – 1 am

MARKETS & FOOD AREAS

**TSUKIJI WHOLESALE MARKET
AND FISH MARKET**
Tsukiji 5-2-1, Chuo-ku, Tokio 104-0045
Station: Tsukiji (Metro: Hibiya line),
Tsukijishijo (Metro: Oedo line)
Open: Mon-Sat, 5 am – 2 pm (fish market 9 am)

MEMORY LANE
Omoide-Yokocho
Nishishinjuku 1-1-1, Shinjuku-ku,
Tokio 160-0023
Station: Shinjuku (Train: JR Yamanote line,
Metro: Marunouchi line)
Open daily: 5 pm – 11 pm

SHINBASHI YURAKUCHO GADO-SHITA
Shinbashi, Minato-ku, Uchisaiwaicho
and Yurakucho, Chiyoda-ku, Tokio
Station: Hibiya (Metro: Hibiya line
and Chiyoda line)
Open daily: 5 pm – 11 pm

COMMUNE 246
Minamiaoyama 3-13, Minato-ku,
Tokyo 107-0062
Station: Omotesando (Metro: Ginza line,
Hanzomon line and Chiyoda line)
Open daily: 11 am – 10 pm

FOOD TRUCKS
Tokyo kokusai forum, Marunouchi 3-5-1,
Chiyoda-ku, Tokio 100-0005
Station: Yurakucho (Train: JR Yamanote line
and JR Keihin-Tohoku line)
Open: Mon-Fri, 11.30 am – 2 pm

KITCHEN SUPPLIES
Kappabashi Dori, Matsugaya 3-8-12,
Taito-ku, Tokio 111-0036
Station: Asakusa (Train: Tsukuba express),
Iriya (Metro: Hibiya line)
Open: Mon-Sat, 9 am – 5 pm

AMEYOKO MARKT
Ameya-Yokocho
Ueno 4, Taito-ku, Tokio 110-0005
Station: Okachimachi (Train: JR Yamanote line
and JR Keihin-Tohoku line)
Open daily: 10 am – 8 pm

EBISU-YOKOCHO
Ebisu 1-7-4, Shibuya-ku, Tokio 150-0013
Station: Ebisu (Train: JR Yamanote line,
JR Saikyo line and JR Syonanshinjuku line)
Open daily: 11 am – 4 am

HAMONIKA-YOKOCHO
Kichijojihoncho 1-31-6, Musashino-shi,
Tokio 180-0004
Station: Kichijoji
(Train: JR Chuo line and JR Somu line)
Open daily: 5 pm – midnight

TOKYO FOOD SHOW
Shibuya 2-24-1, Shibuya-ku,
Tokio 150-0002
Station: Shibuya (Train: JR Yamanote line,
JR Saikyo line, JR Syonanshinjuku line and
Keio-Inogashira line)
Open daily: 10 am – 9 pm

HIROSHIMA

Savoury Japanese pancakes with cabbage
(Hiroshima-style okonomiyaki)
OKONOMI-MURA
Shintenchi 5-13, Naka-ku,
Hiroshima 730-0034
Station: Hatchobori
(Tram: Hiroshimadentetsu line)
Open daily: 11.30 am – midnight

Japanese-style grilled eel / conger eel
(unagi / anago no kabayaki)
UENO ANAGOMESHI
Miyajimaguchi 1-5-11, Hatsukaichi,
Hiroshima 739-0411
Station: Miyajimaguchi
(Train: JR Sanyohonsen line)
Open: 10 am – 7 pm

MARKETS & FOOD AREAS

MIYAJIMA STREET FOOD MARKET
Miyajimachō 838, Hatsukaichi,
Hiroshima 739-0588
Station: Miyajima (Ferry from Miyajimaguchi
station on JR Sanyohonsen line)
Open: 8 am – 5 pm

OSAKA

Monaka with mascarpone / Matcha latte
OSAKA CHAKAI
Tenjinbashi 2-1-25-1F, Kita-ku,
Osaka 530-0041
Station: Tenjinbashisuji Rokuchome
(Metro: Tanimashi line and Sakaisuji line)
Open daily: 9 am – 11 pm

Japanese omelette / Soy milk pudding
MAEDA TOFU
Tenjinbashi 3-4-9, Kita-ku,
Osaka 530-0041
Station: Tenjinbashisuji Rokuchome
(Metro: Tanimashi line and Sakaisuji line)
Open daily: Mon-Sat, 11 am – 7 pm

Tripe
TSUGIE
Tenjinbashi 5-6-33, Kita-ku,
Osaka 530-0041
Station: Tenma (Train: JR Kanjo line)
Open daily: 5 pm – midnight

Crab and scallops with ponzu
TOYO
Higashinodamachi 3-2-26, Miyakojima-ku,
Osaka 534-0024
Station: Kyobashi (Train: JR Kanjo line)
Open: Tues-Sat, 3.30 pm – 9 pm

Deep-fried skewered meat and vegetables
(kushikatsu)
YAEKATSU
Ebisu Higashi 3-4-13, Naniwa-ku,
Osaka 556-0002
Station: Dobutsuenmae
(Metro: Midosuji line) and Shin-imamiya
(Train: JR Kanjo line)
Open: 10.30 am – 9.30 pm
(closed Thursdays and third Wednesday)

Octopus balls (takoyaki)
HANADAKO
Kakuda-cho 9-16, Kita-ku, Osaka 530-0017
Station: Osaka (JR: Kanjko line) and Umeda
(Metro: Midosuji line)
Open daily: 10 am – 11 pm

Savoury Japanese pancakes with cabbage
(Osaka-style okonomiyaki)
ZOUYA
Tamade Nishi 2-7-10, Nishinari-ku,
Osaka 530-0017
Station: Tamade (Metro: Yotsubashi line)
Open: Tues-Sat, 5 pm – 11 pm, Sundays and
holidays, 3 pm – 11 pm

MARKETS & FOOD AREAS

TENJINBASHISUJI-SHOTENGAI
Tenjinbashi, Kita-ku, Osaka 530-0041
Station: Tenjinbashisuji Rokuchome
(Metro: Tanimashi line and Sakaisuji line)
Open: 9 am – 8 pm

KOREAN TOWN
Tsuruhashi 1, Ikuno-ku, Osaka 544-0031
Station: Tsuruhashi (Train: JR Kanjo line and
Kintetsu Osaka line, metro: Sennichimae line)
Open: 10 am – 11 pm

KUROMON MARKET
KUROMON ICHIBA MARKET
Nipponbashi 2-4-1, Chuo-ku,
Osaka 542-0073
Station: Nipponbashi
(Metro: Sennichimae line and Sakaisuji line)
Open: 9 am – 6 pm

TENMA FOOD AREA
Nishiki-cho, Kita-ku, Osaka 530-0034
Station: Tenma (Train: JR Kanjo line)
Open: 11 am – 11 pm

FUKUSHIMA STANDING BARS
Fukushima, Fukushima-ku, Osaka 553-0003
Station: Fukushima (Train: JR Kanjo line)
Open: 11.30 am – midnight

SHINSEKAI-SHOTENGAI
Ebisubashi 1, Naniwa-ku, Osaka 556-0002
Station: Dobutsuenmae (Metro: Midosuji line)
and Shin-imamiya (Train: JR Kanjo line)
Open: 10 am – midnight

FUKUOKA

Fried skewered chicken (yakitori)
KAWAYA
Shirogane 1-15-7, Chuo-ku,
Fukuoka 810-0012
Station: Yakuin (Metro: Nanakumasen)
Open daily: 5 pm – midnight

Pesto Ramen
RAMEN UNARI
Nakasu 3-6-23, Hakata-ku,
Fukuoka 810-0801
Station: Nakasukawabata (Metro: Kuko line)
Open: Mon-Sat, 6 pm – 6 am

Ramen with pork stock (tonkotsu ramen)
GANSO NAGAHAMAYA
Nagahama 2-5-38, Chuo-ku,
Fukuoka 810-0072
Station: Akasaka (Metro: Kuko line)
Open daily: 4 am – 1:45 am

Omelette on fried rice (omuraisu)
GOKOKU
Akasaka 1F 2-1-8, Chuo-ku,
Fukuoka 810-0042
Station: Akasaka (Metro: Kuko line)
Open: Tues-Sun, 11 am – 9.30 pm

MARKETS & FOOD AREAS

YATAI FOOD CARTS
Tenjin 2, Chuo-ku, Fukuoka 810-0001
Station: Tenjin (Metro: Kuko line)
Open daily: 6 pm – 2 am

MINOSHIMA-SHOTENGAI
Minoshima 1-17-15, Hakata-ku,
Fukuoka 812-0017
Station: Hakata (Train: JR Hakataminami line,
JR Sasaguri line, JR Kagoshima line)

OKAYAMA

Tofu dishes
OKABE
Omote-cho 1-10-1, Kita-ku,
Okayama 700-0822
Station: Kenchodori
(Tram from Okayama station:
Okayamadenkikido)
Open: Mon-Weds/Fri-Sat, 11.30 am – 2 pm

Udon noodles with oysters
KORAKUEN
South entrance, Korakuen 1-5, Kita-ku,
Okayama 703-8257
Station: Korakuenmae
(Bus from Okayama station:
Okayamadenkikido)
Open daily: 10 am – 6 pm

INDEX

A

52 Thick pancakes with sweetened **adzuki beans** DORAYAKI
129 Cake with sweetened **adzuki beans** TAIYAKI
206 Sweetened **adzuki beans** TSUBUAN
207 Rice cake filled with sweetened **adzuki beans** DAIFUKU
60 Grilled **aubergine** with bonito flakes YAKI NASU
161 European/Dutch-style **aubergines** (eggplant) NASU NO ORANDANI

B

31 Octopus **balls** TAKOYAKI
59 Tofu **balls** with thick dashi sauce TOFU-DANGO NO ANKAKE
202 Marinated **bamboo shoots** MENMA
124 Curry **bread** with beef CURRY PAN
140 Thinly sliced **beef** with egg GYUNIKU NO TAMAGO-TOJI
60 Grilled aubergine with **bonito flakes** YAKI NASU
124 Curry bread with **beef** CURRY PAN
126 Steamed **bun** NIKUMAN
184 Scampi **burger** EBIKATSU BURGER
203 Shiitake-seaweed **butter** SHIITAKE AONORI BUTTER

C

134 Savoury Japanese pancakes with **cabbage** (Hiroshima-style) OKONOMIYAKI (HIROSHIMA-YAKI)
177 Savoury Japanese pancakes with **cabbage** (Osaka-style) OKONOMIYAKI (OSAKA-STYLE)
129 **Cake** with sweetened adzuki beans TAIYAKI
27 Breaded **chicken** CHICKEN KATSU
55 Marinated and fried **chicken** TORI NO KARAAGE
65 Triangular breaded **chicken** sandwich CHICKEN KATSU SANDO
80 Fried skewered **chicken** YAKITORI (NEGIMA)
158 Okra and **chicken** salad OKURA TO TORINIKU NO SALADA
200 **Chicken** stock TORIGARA SOUP
51 Pickled **Chinese cabbage** HAKUSAI NO TSUKEMONO
38 Miso soup with **clams** ASARI NO MISOSHIRU
104 **Cod roe** tempura with perilla leaves MENTAIKO TO SHISO NO TEMPURA
41 Fishcake with **corn** TOMORO-KOSHI NO SATSUMA-AGE
178 **Crab** and scallops with ponzu (Japanese citrus soy sauce) KANI TO HOTATE NO PONZU GAKE
154 Japanese-style **croquettes** with minced meat NIKU KOROKKE
34 **Cucumber** with spicy miso dip MOROKYU
37 Japanese **curry** with vegetables YASAI CURRY
124 **Curry** bread with beef CURRY PAN

D

83 **Daikon**, egg and fishcake in stock ODEN
187 Rice with sea bream sashimi and hot **dashi** TAI CHAZUKE
59 Tofu balls with thick **dashi** sauce TOFU-DANGO NO ANKAKE
69 Don (rice bowl) with yuba and thick **dashi** sauce YUBA NO DONBURI
28 Ice-cold soba noodles with **dipping sauce** ZARU SOBA
202 Gyoza **dipping sauce** GYOZA NO TARE
120 Fried and steamed **dumplings** GYOZA

E

130 Japanese-style grilled **eel** UNAGI / ANAGO NO KABAYAKI
83 Daikon, **egg** and fishcake in stock ODEN
140 Thinly sliced beef with **egg** GYUNIKU NO TAMAGO-TOJI
153 Smoked **eggs** KUNSEI TAMAGO

F

42 Sushi balls topped with **fish** NIGIRI SUSHI
41 **Fishcake** with corn TOMORO-KOSHI NO SATSUMA-AGE
83 Daikon, egg and **fishcake** in stock ODEN

G

95 Sardines with **ginger** IWASHI NO NITSUKE
146 Cold **green tea** TSUMETAI RYOKUCHA
149 Shaved ice with **green tea** syrup MATCHA KAKIGORI
151 Japanese **green tea** latte MATCHA LATTE
202 **Gyoza** dipping sauce GYOZA NO TARE

H

167 Rice with **hijiki** seaweed HIJIKI GOHAN

K

199 **Katsuobushi** salt KATSUOBUSHI-JIO
170 Pork and **kimchi** stir-fry BUTA KIMCHI

M

190 Grilled **mackerel** with sea salt SABA NO SHIOYAKI
150 Monaka with **mascarpone** MASCARPONE NO MONAKA
79 Deep-fried skewered **meat** and vegetables KUSHIKATSU
99 **Meatballs** in sweet sauce NIKUDANGO NO ANKAKE
48 Ramen with spicy minced **meat** TANTANMEN
154 Japanese-style croquettes with **minced meat** NIKU KOROKKE
169 **Miso**-marinated and baked salmon SAKE NO SAIKYO YAKI
34 Cucumber with spicy **miso** dip MOROKYU
204 Concentrated **miso sauce** MISODARE
38 **Miso soup** with clams ASARI NO MISOSHIRU
150 **Monaka** with mascarpone MASCARPONE NO MONAKA

N

113 Dipping **noodles** TSUKEMEN
173 Fried rice and **noodles** SOBAMESHI

O

31 **Octopus** balls TAKOYAKI
158 **Okra** and chicken salad OKURA TO TORINIKU NO SALADA
91 **Omelette** on fried rice OMARAISU

162 Japanese **omelette** DASHIMAKI TAMAGO
73 Udon noodles with **oysters** KAKI UDON

P

52 Thick **pancakes** with sweetened azuki beans DORAYAKI
134 Savoury Japanese **pancakes** with cabbage (Hiroshima-style) OKONOMIYAKI (HIROSHIMA-YAKI)
177 Savoury Japanese **pancakes** with cabbage (Osaka-style) OKONOMIYAKI (OSAKA-STYLE)
104 Cod roe tempura with **perilla leaves** MENTAIKO TO SHISO NO TEMPURA
111 **Pesto** ramen BASIL RAMEN
204 Concentrated **pesto sauce** BASILDARE
178 Crab and scallops with **ponzu** (Japanese citrus soy sauce) KANI TO HOTATE NO PONZU GAKE
170 **Pork** and kimchi stir-fry BUTA KIMCHI
174 Sweet and sour **pork** SUBUTA
203 Marinated braised **pork** CHASHU
88 Ramen with **pork stock** TONKOTSU RAMEN
103 **Potato** salad POTETO SALADA
157 Soy milk **pudding** TONYU PURIN

R

48 **Ramen** with spicy minced meat TANTANMEN
87 Vegetarian **ramen** VEGE RAMEN
88 **Ramen** with pork stock TONKOTSU RAMEN
111 Pesto **ramen** BASIL RAMEN
200 Vegetarian **ramen stock** VEGE RAMEN NO SOUP
91 Omelette on fried **rice** OMARAISU
167 **Rice** with hijiki seaweed HIJIKI GOHAN
173 Fried **rice** and noodles SOBAMESHI
187 **Rice** with sea bream sashimi and hot dashi TAI CHAZUKE
198 Cooked **rice** HAKUMAI
189 Hand-rolled **rice balls** with salmon SAKE NO ONIGIRI
69 Don (**rice bowl**) with yuba and thick dashi sauce YUBA NO DONBURI
92 Sashimi on **rice bowl** KAISEN-DON
195 Karaage-don (**rice bowl**) with salsa SALSA SOSU NO KARAAGE DON
207 **Rice cake** filled with sweetened adzuki beans DAIFUKU

S

103 Potato **salad** POTETO SALADA
158 Okra and chicken **salad** OKURA TO TORINIKU NO SALADA
169 Miso-marinated and baked **salmon** SAKE NO SAIKYO YAKI
189 Hand-rolled rice balls with **salmon** SAKE NO ONIGIRI
195 Karaage-don (rice bowl) with **salsa** SALSA SOSU NO KARAAGE DON
204 Concentrated **salt sauce** SHIODARE
65 Triangular breaded chicken **sandwich** CHICKEN KATSU SANDO
95 **Sardines** with ginger IWASHI NO NITSUKE
92 **Sashimi** on rice bowl KAISEN-DON
187 Rice with sea bream **sashimi** and hot dashi TAI CHAZUKE
56 Grilled scallops with **soy sauce** and butter HOTATE NO GRILL
178 Crab and **scallops** with ponzu (Japanese citrus soy sauce) KANI TO HOTATE NO PONZU GAKE
184 **Scampi** burger EBIKATSU BURGER
187 Rice with **sea bream** sashimi and hot dashi TAI CHAZUKE
190 Grilled mackerel with **sea salt** SABA NO SHIOYAKI
203 **Shiitake**-seaweed butter SHIITAKE AONORI BUTTER
96 **Spinach** with sesame sauce HORENSO NO GOMAAE
183 Green **soy bean** shake EDAMAME SHAKE
149 Shaved ice with green tea syrup MATCHA KAKIGORI
203 **Shiitake**-seaweed butter SHIITAKE AONORI BUTTER
28 Ice-cold **soba noodles** with dipping sauce ZARU SOBA
183 Green **soy bean** shake EDAMAME SHAKE
202 Eggs in **soy sauce** TAMAGO NO SHOYUZUKE
157 **Soy milk** pudding TONYU PURIN

56 Grilled scallops with **soy sauce** and butter HOTATE NO GRILL
70 Cold tofu with various types of garnish and **soy sauce** HI YAYAKKO
96 Spinach with **sesame sauce** HORENSO NO GOMAAE
123 Japanese **sponge cake** KASUTERA
145 **Steak** with Japanese savoury sauce GYU STEEKI WAFU-SOSU
83 Daikon, egg and fishcake in **stock** ODEN
196 Japanese **stock** DASHI
42 **Sushi balls** topped with fish NIGIRI SUSHI
199 **Sushi rice** SUSHI MESHI
174 **Sweet and sour** pork SUBUTA
149 Shaved ice with green tea **syrup** MATCHA KAKIGORI

T

204 Concentrated **tantan sauce** TANTANDARE
59 **Tofu balls** with thick dashi sauce TOFU-DANGO NO ANKAKE
66 Vegetables with "broken" **tofu** YASAI NO SHIRAAE
70 Cold **tofu** with various types of garnish and soy sauce HI YAYAKKO
203 **Tonkatsu sauce** TONKATSU-SOSU

U

73 **Udon** noodles with oysters KAKI UDON

V

37 Japanese curry with **vegetables** YASAI CURRY
66 **Vegetables** with "broken" tofu YASAI NO SHIRAAE
79 Deep-fried skewered meat and **vegetables** KUSHIKATSU

Y

69 Don (rice bowl) with **yuba** and thick dashi sauce YUBA NO DONBURI

COLOPHON

www.lannoo.com
Register on our website and we will regularly send you a newsletter with information about new books and exciting exclusive offers.

With special thanks to Katia Vlerick for editing the texts.

TEXT
Tom Vandenberghe
www.eetavontuur.be, www.eetramen.be & www.eethaven.be
Miho Shibuya & Tomoko Kaji
www.gohan.be

PHOTOGRAPHY AND FOOD STYLING
Luk Thys
www.foodphoto.be

DESIGN
Klaartje De Buck, Letterwerf

TRANSLATION
Claire Singleton

CHECK OUT
www.ilikestreetfood.com

If you have any observations or questions, please contact our editorial office: redactielifestyle@lannoo.com.

© Uitgeverij Lannoo nv, Tielt, 2017
D/2017/45/417 – NUR 442
ISBN: 978 94 014 3757 8

All rights reserved. No part of this book may be reproduced, stored in a retrieval system, or transmitted in any form or by any means, electronic, electrostatic, magnetic tape, mechanical, photocopying, recording or otherwise, without the prior permission in writing of the publisher.